Kiwi-nomics

Conversations with New Zealand's Economic Soul

Viv Grigg

Urban Leadership Foundation

Auckland, New Zealand

Some other books by Viv Grigg

Companion to the Poor, tr. *Siervos Entre os Pobres* (Portuguese),
Servos Entre Los Povres (Spanish),
Mit Dem Arben Leben (German), also in Korean and Tamil
Cry of the Urban Poor. tr. *O Grito dos Pobres* (Portuguese).
Towards an Auckland Business Theology
Transforming Cities: An Urban Leadership Guide
The Kingdom of God and Land Rights
The Spirit of Christ and Postmodern City

ISBN: 978-0-9582019-0-2

Published by:

Urban Leadership Foundation

P. O. Box 68-244, Newton, Auckland

www.urbanleaders.org

Dedication

To my my three kids:

Leonardo, Bianca and Monique;
the author, the creative, the internationalist.
May they find in these musings passion for creating poetry,
celebrating life, and doing justice.

And to their gracious, sensitive, creative mother, Iêda,

Gifted preacher, mother and hospital chaplain, who has journeyed
with me through entrepreneurship of multiple organisations, living
on manna from heaven, in poverty and in wealth, in years of hard
labour and in periods of rest, and stayed with me when my eyes glaze
over as new themes echo through my mind.

Economic Discipleship

1. Love
- Work of Individual
- Social Responsibility

2. Creativity
- Innovation
- Entrepreneurship
- Technology

3. Productivity
- Wealth Creation
- God's Blessing — Prosperity
- Profitability

4. Cooperation
- Social Responsibility
  - Reconciliation
  - Alienation
- Fair Trade
- Class Struggle
  - Trade Unions

5. Work and Rest
- Sabbath — Creation Care
- Jubilee — Ecological Gospel
- Manna — Christian Work

6. Simplicity
- Renunciation
- Detachment
- Dangers of Wealth

7. Redistribution
- Deacons
- Tithing — Giving
- Equity
- Equality — Poverty
  - Non-Destitute Poverty
  - Social Justice

8. Management
- Debt — Savings
- Budgeting
  - Partnerships
  - Sustainability
  - Accounting
  - Investment

9. Ownership
- Private Ownership
  - Land Rights
  - Asset Sales
  - Resisting Globalization
  - One World Government
- State Ownership

10. Freedom
- from Slavery
- for Worship
- from overbureaucracy to to business

Table of Contents

Table of Figures

Introducing the Conversationalists...

The sun beat down on the galvanised iron roof of my room in a Philippine slum in 1978. The afternoon siesta turned into a time of writing as I conversed with the horrors of poverty into which the Lord had led me. This conversation began with extending my Navigator training in discipleship into three articles on the cross in Luke 14, one on *Discipleship and Possessions*. A Colonel working for President Marcos, a Catholic liberationist nun, a Marxist were my debating companions in a class on national development at the University of the Philippines - all seeking ways to bring about a philosophy of economic development– all passionate, each to his own. I wrote profusely to develop a *Biblical Framework of Development* in response.

I wandered on a motorbike teaching these themes across the New Zealand revival in 1981-2 and 1985-6, seeking to help people respond from affluence to poverty, publishing some in *Companion to the Poor*. This conversation touched the revival. It was a communal conversation. Some churches and leaders began to implement *Kingdom Economics* principles. Tom Marshall at Waikanae, Bryan Hathaway at Te Atatu, Murray Robertson in Spreydon, Bernie Ogilvie with YWAM, Bruce MacDonald with Whakatane New Life, the Apostolic churches and others developed these themes into processes. Judy Yule expanded similar themes through Tear Fund.

I then returned to the slums. The last three decades of training of hundreds of slum pastors in cities round the globe through story-telling consultations has required constant reflection on these ideas in both theory and practice.

Other conversations have interfaced. Microenterprise began developing as a discipline round 1975, when I first went to the slums. Some conversations are historical. I early had stumbled on the cooperative principles popularised by Raushenbusch whose Social Gospel transformed America and Kagawa of Japan, who transformed Japan. Some are polemic debates between ethicists and economists. Former Catholic priest turned economist, Michael Novak in *The Spirit of Democratic Capitalism* and Peter Berger, the sociologist, in *The Capitalist Revolution; Fifty Propositions About Prosperity, Equality and Liberty*, opened new fields in terms of the moral principles inherent in socialised

1

Capitalism. Listening to Alan Greenspan on audiobook for hours on his role in superintending the US Federal Reserve and keeping the US economy stable, gave some degree of insight into the economic crisis - but the recent movies on the theme are easier to digest, if not exactly full of morality.

More recently, training of students who teach these themes in the slums, has enabled feedback from their internships in self-help groups and microfinance in the slums. This has expanded the sense of how the poor can escape from poverty. That cannot be done without education, so commencing slum schools occurs. And advocacy to change the structures of oppression becomes critical – particularly when dealing with access to ownership of land, the bedrock of Capitalism.

One sadness each time back home from my missionary exploits has been observing the disjointed New Zealand conversation. We have needed collectively-owned Biblical ways of relating to macro-economic issues. Perhaps my Baptist understanding of the very nature of the church should affirm an understanding that salt and light bubble up from the voices of the people, not down through hierarchies. On the other hand, even though Christendom has collapsed, the state-church denominations contributed serious reflective voices, significant being Richard Randerson, and Ruth Smithies.[1]

Meanwhile, the grassroots explosion of charismatic and Pentecostal churches advanced an imported American *prosperity theology*, which has resulted in nothing except pain for those who followed it.

Bryan Johnson walked with me for some years training leaders in these principles in the slums. Fifty of my MA in Transformational Urban Leadership students have been doing the same, along with a number of the sixty professors in the eight partner programs we have catalysed around the world in the *MA in Transformational Urban Leadership*.[2] Other leaders of *Urban Poor Learning Networks* have multiplied these with their slum pastors in multiple cities particularly out from Hyderabad and Kampala.

Where Are We Going?

The aim of this book is two-fold.

1. To lay a basis for churches across New Zealand to develop Economic Discipleship training as part of the global movement towards Economic Discipleship. To accomplish the first half of this the book is a conversation starter of simple Biblical truths

2. To establish the basis for conversations at policy levels between Christian leaders, theologians and economists.

Part 1 browses through six periods in redemption history: Genesis, the Jubilee, the Prophets, Jesus, The Acts Community, and Paul's epistles, identifying ten economic principles and looking at their manifestation at each phase of Biblical history.

These are then integrated into some Biblical theology themes. The Jubilee theme is integrated into a Biblical theology in Part 1. In part 2, we further integrate some Biblical theologies: management principles; cooperation and cooperative economic structures as alternatives to Capitalism; creativity that leads to innovation and entrepreneurship; land rights and land ownership and do some initial engagement to the New Zealand context.

In Part 3, the conversation moves from the Biblical conversation to the global and national economic conversations. Instead of beginning with the Bible, the issues become the starting point, and are examined from a Biblical perspective. The questions are raised as to how these Biblical principles apply to global political economic systems (Capitalism, Socialism, mixed economies). These are applied to some specific issues of globalisation. What is their impact on the present loss of New Zealand's ownership of banking systems, and asset sales? What is the likely impact on New Zealand's survival with the upcoming trade agreement? What is the needed Christian voice?

This is not a comprehensive analysis of all the economic issues in New Zealand. Migration, housing, the elderly, ethnicity and poverty, social welfare, education as right not commodity, and much more - are significant agendas for economics, and feature highly in various policy analysis documents in a highly researched society. These chapters are small conversation starters in some arenas, seeking to demonstrate an approach of applying Biblical theology to the issues.

This is not a heavy theological study – you can find those in the bibliography. Nor is it a course in economics. Rather, it is a simple summary of some key Biblical themes and an initial engagement of these with some current economic and financial themes, an introduction to a conversation, whereby we can bring the principles of the Kingdom of God into the economics of our nation.

This book is not primarily for businessmen who live in the world of making money (though they may find it of great value), as there are many books written about business principles from a Christian perspective.[3] It is also not a study on social policy or how to deliver social work programs for the destitute – the members of the *Council of Christian Social Services* is constantly addressing such issues across New Zealand.

The concluding call to action and the appendices map some ways forward for local churches, clusters of leaders in cities, and at national levels.

Thoughts on Theological Style

Few Christian economists stand in the arena as overtly Christian (though a good number are Christian), as the discipline is supposedly neutral towards religious or moral beliefs, it seems important to write up the years of reflection on economic theologies in a popular manner for churches. But the complexity of economics means that this has to oscillate in an academic manner for those Christians in leadership roles in the nation.

There are some essential processes as to how to develop such practical theological reflection based on the scriptures, sometimes known as a hermeneutic approach. The urban hermeneutics used here are developed in depth, in my works on *Transformational Conversations*.[4] I developed this in an earlier book for New Zealand, *The Spirit of Christ and the Postmodern City*.

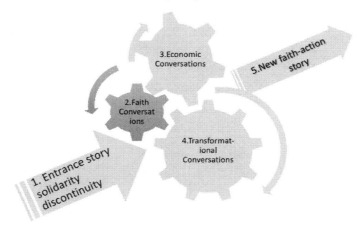

Figure 1: The Transformational Conversations process engaging theology and national economic conversations.

The issues in focus are derived first from encounters, or the *discontinuities* within our current context, or our solidarity with those in pain and *the urban or national conversations* that these evoke. Such things as the anger at a government pawning our national forests or the dispossession of a factory owner with a hundred workers because with the slash of a pen his prime minster has flooded the country with cheap Chinese shoes. Such injustices force us into social and economic analysis, the *economic conversation*.

Out of the anger, the discontinuities, the pain, comes the *theological conversation* in this work, the reflection on the issues from the scriptures. These are based on an approach of what is known as Biblical Theology, looking at theological themes across the whole of the scriptures. One first needs to look at those themes within the context of each Biblical writer, not just a way of pulling texts willy-nilly out of context. There are thirteen major themes that have been used as significant integrators of Biblical theology.

In this study, the overarching theme utilized is the Kingdom of God,[5] commonly utilized by many movements in history (e.g. Calvin, the World Council of Churches, Catholicism, Presbyterian theologies…), and central to Jesus teachings. This theme subsumes Creation, Fall, Redemption and Consummation. It is manifested in covenants so subsumes Covenantal Theology. It has different manifestations in the different ages of Redemption History, so subsumes classic Dispensationalism with its seven ages popularized by the Schofield Bible of Fundamentalism (particularly popular among Brethren in New Zealand), while creating a better balance of many of its teachings. Under this rubric of the Kingdom we can engage the social, economic, political and environmental dimensions of life. This study concentrates on fifty economic principles across Redemption History, coalescing them into ten themes.

The synthesis of the dialogue between these conversations I have called the *Transformational Conversation*. That conversation is mediated into society through *conversational structures*, organisations or movements built around these principles that represent the voice of scriptures. For Biblical truth requires a call to action, to repentance, to change, it is never simply ideas. Action is collective, and *social repentance* is needed if we are to redeem a very lost nation. A hermeneutic without action is incestuous theological nonsense.

Communication of truth requires *simplicity*, and that is best done with *slogans, mnemonics, parables* and simple references to scriptures rather than communicating extensive Hebrew or Greek exegetical processes and referring to extensive theological debates. In this work, the importance of simplicity in teaching Biblical economics puts constraints as to the academic referencing in the text. So this work may not satisfy theologians. One pet peeve of theologians is proof texting (simply referencing ideas to texts without reviewing their original context) – yet simple Biblical texts are the basis for many in their Bible Studies, and as this has grown from conversations at the grassroots, I have not been afraid to keep these in the footnotes.

Our means of communicating of perhaps fifty principles of the scriptures, is a reduction to ten core economic principles. Reductionist slogans, mnemonics, stories, parables is the environment in which I live, as I engage with some of the two billion urban poor who are oral learners, so this technique is five principles on each hand – the most that many of us can remember. Other principles are subsumed in these.

> ### *Celebrating Economics*
>
> I was recently teaching these ten principles in one of the early churches I had helped found in the slums of Manila. At each step, each principle, there was a silent clatter of enthusiastic discussion among the people, as for thirty-five years they had tracked the development of these principles, one by one! We rote repeated the first five principles on one hand, the second on the other hand, as you would in preschool! They left, celebrating teachings that they knew had set them free!

While I have not gone into the depths of exegesis in this written book, such exegesis over the years underlies simplicity. If one is interested in the complexity of Biblical underpinnings, they may find resource articles in the Bibliography.

In the latter chapters, where we interface theology with complex national and international economics, the discussion is more complex by necessity. This twelfth, greatly expanded, double in length, edition of this work, indicates the ever evolving nature of the conversations – particularly with the TPPA (Trans Pacific Partnership Agreement).

Contribution of Kiwinomics[6]

There are many attempts by theologians to integrate faith and economics - historically and in the present era. This study seeks to create a simple framework for (1) the individual, (2) family, (3) faith community, (4) nation and (5) global economics so as to biblically evaluate their economic lives and infrastructures in which they live. Simple frameworks multiply teachings.

In terms of the *economic conversation*, I claim no particular expertise in the economic field, but because of the nature of being called to be among the poor, I have been forced for years to stumble through various development economics papers filled with jargon that only an elite economic priesthood might understand. This book contains no new economic theories, though I trust I represent existing theory fairly, if simply. Rather, the focus is on Biblical theology as it impinges on the economists' domain – expecting that they are the technical specialists and a response is needed from them in the process of interpreting the principles of scripture into the principles of their discipline. This study is not espousing specific policies, but does open the basis for conversations that critique some and affirm others.

Think-Tanks in Middle Earth

We may link these ideas to a historic Anglican approach of *middle axioms* used as a basis for developing pronouncements by gatherings of church leaders on economic issues.[7]

For churches without the hierarchy, structure and education of the mainline denominations, this becomes more complicated, as the locus of authority of any voice is dispersed by virtue of belief in the equality of all believers – all hobbits are of equal value, no? But ecumenical consultations and think-tanks can be used to accomplish similar goals, and in New Zealand, *VisionNetwork* has a mandate from many churches and denominations to accomplish this.

Such consultations among leaders in the slums have been the basis of this study, hence its simplicity in the early chapters, as *a theology of the people*.[8] In the latter chapters, engagement with the economic systems requires think-tanks of well-trained economists working with theologians. politicians and social activists to determine appropriate courses of action.

Presuppositions

This implies that it is valid to engage economic theories with Biblical truths. The key is in our commitment to the historic Christian beliefs that the Bible is truth as an entity, and/or contains truth, and/or is our final measure for faith and practice. My own stance is based on the Bible's historicity: the fulfilment of over six hundred prophecies; its standing the test of time as the basis of truth and faith; its superior morality; but ultimately to personally testing its truths and promises again and again by walking out on limbs into the darkest places of earth then watching him act around me, as many multitudes have done through the centuries. It is confirmed when I watch these economic teachings transform the lives of poor people. Such belief is intensely rational.

On the flip side, are economic theories truth? Again, within the discipline there are tests for veracity and validity of its theories. There is a pragmatism in economics where consistent performance validates a theory – until it fails and is replaced. That pragmatic rationality finds itself short facing global

7

issues that depend on morality and ethics. For economics as a discipline is known for its reductionism and frequent inability to adapt to social realities, beyond the purity of the economic issues. Its emptiness in such arenas requires this kind of engagement with a morality that is referenced back to an infinite personality undergirding the structures of the universe – only fools do not seek the One.

A Communal Pilgrimage

These theological ideas have been tested by leaders teaching them and adding to them: Pr. P.K. Moses in Hyderabad; Pr. John Baptist Lukwago in Kampala; Pr. Alvin Mbola in Nairobi; Rev. Paul Turner in Los Angeles. 53 MATUL students and many pastors in Delhi, Kolkata, Chennai, Nagpur, Rio de Janeiro, Manila, Bangkok, Mozambique, Kampala, Nairobi have debated these ideas over enthusiastic global internet classes early morning and late night, and r teaching among the urban poor. My daughter, Monique Wike, edited out the worst grammar. Thomas Chacko, a NZ economist and a wise advisor, has kept me from some more extreme statements in my semi-literate state regarding the complexities of economics. Azusa Pacific University graciously allotted some units for research and writing in 2015-6. My father, grandfather and great-great-grandfather's examples of national leadership in their professions - based on their sense of godly duty to an emergent nation - give meaning to speaking prophetically to our nation.

Viv Grigg

International Director, Urban Leadership Foundation, Auckland, June 2016

Go to Kiwinomics Facebook page to submit responses, corrections, additions, reflections, opposition, wisdom, modification, extensions, explanations, curiosity. Kiwinomics.org is the associated website.

Economic Discipleship is developed in much greater breadth at www.urbanleaders.org/560CommEcon An online version is being developed at www.economicdiscipleship.online

Prelude: The First Principle: Economics as Love

The day we meet and fall in love with Jesus Christ, we find a passion that fires all of our life and meshes us with the integrator of the universe. His love enfolds us in a grip that will not let us go. Embraced in such love, we in turn, press into loving all, to the depth of our capacity, to the breadth of our capacity.

The integrator of the universe, however, expresses his love in concrete economic terms. As it flows through us, we find expressions of his love in economics. Love for family is manifest in fatherly and motherly provision of necessities. Love for community is expressed in the provision of employment for as many as our giftedness can sustain. Love for the nation is expressed in just, productive, creative, liberating economics.

Because God is a community in unity, God is love. His love is reflected in our individual humanness as we act justly in financial areas. As his love is reflected in our communal humanity, we develop co-operative economics. This is a core theme throughout this material. As love disappears in societies, economics becomes exploitive, dehumanised and lacking in morality.

Such love is released where the Holy Spirit moves freely. Where revivals occur, the love of the Holy Spirit overwhelms many. There are immediate economic changes that occur. Families become whole, sins are put away, unjust and sordid businesses disappear. As revivals die, the distance between people increases, sins against others and society increase, civility in society and the public square becomes rudeness, and economics begin to disintegrate. But such economic change is largely determined by the theology preceding a revival. I would commend the teachings in this book as some patterns of theology that perhaps may be a basis for the next wave of revival across post-modern youth of New Zealand.

Part 1: Ten Principles of Economic Discipleship

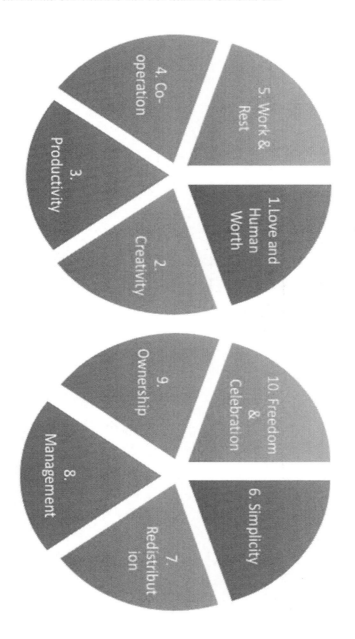

Figure 2: Ten principles of economic discipleship.

1. Responding to the Issues of our Times

My deaf neighbour lost his job of ten years. My newly graduated friends cannot find fitting work for a graduate. Another friend quietly became unemployed.

Recession? Depression? Economic collapse? The Biblical concept of famine in an agricultural society seems remarkably like our current context. Many are anxious during this economic crisis - there seems to be one every two or three years! But famines are ancient, and the ancient wisdom of God's response is well tested. *Those who put their trust in the Lord, shall lack for no good thing.*[1]

Did you know that Isaac sowed during a time of famine and reaped a hundred fold?

> *And there was a famine in the land. Then Isaac sowed in that land, and received in the same year a hundredfold: and the Lord blessed him.*[2]

That is because there are Biblical mysteries, economic themes that protect us during such times. But lacking education in scriptural economics, we live in the world's ways and suffer for our folly!

For other friends in business leadership, the daily pressures of marketing products in a multinational world in order to sustain competitiveness and expand income, keeping the board and investors happy with a reasonable rate of return, is a pressure that weighs on their soul. They need national and international infrastructural support.

And at national levels, for many decades, Christian thinkers have been critiquing the advances and excesses of Capitalism, predicting that areas of violation of divine principles, as with Communism, will eventually lead to catastrophic system meltdowns.

Economic issues are central in Kiwi conversation. So the church must be engaged in bringing Biblical principles into that conversation at multiple levels from daily life to national governance.

Michele Levine, Chief Executive Officer at Roy Morgan says:

> *Economic issues dominate in New Zealand – 44% (up 4% since March 2015) of New Zealanders say the biggest problems facing New Zealand are economic and 32% (up 7%) say economic issues are also the biggest problems facing the World.*

> *In New Zealand the biggest economic issue is Poverty/ The gap between the rich and the poor/ Imbalance of wealth 21% (up 3%) followed by Economy/ Financial crisis/ Recession/ High dollar 10% (up 5%), Unemployment/ Job security 5% (down 3%)... –and Cost of living/ Inflation/ Financial hardship/ Household debt 4% (down 1%).*

Housing shortage/ Housing affordability 14% (up 4%) is a huge problem facing New Zealand – now at a record high… Many Kiwis also view Government/ Politicians/ Leadership/ Government spending 8% (down 1%) as a significant problem.[3]

There has been some teaching on Kingdom Economic principles across the land. This book and conversation integrates these two: the current economic crises and economic issues, and the Biblical teachings that predict them and which bring solutions.

Western socialised Capitalism (also called a mixed economy) includes many aspects of biblical economics, significantly modified toward the good by the values of the Protestant Reformation and the impetus towards integrity, industriousness and equality by the dramatic conversion of millions in the First and Second Great Awakenings. It has, as a system, enabled many millions around the globe to escape poverty over the last century. It has also violated each of the biblical principles documented in the following chapters, and as it has moved into globalised Capitalism, it has created increasing levels of oppression and reversal of the democratisation of wealth central to Biblical teaching.

A U.S. visionary, Bruce Maclaren writes:

The Prosperity Crisis was the key symptom of an unsustainable (or suicidal) system… this unprecedented prosperity has too often been purchased through various kinds of theft.

First, we have stolen resources from the planet at an indefensible rate, stealing from our children and children's children.

Second, we have stolen land from native peoples, and we have stolen resources from nations whose people lack even basic needs (take dirty Coltan exports from Congo in our cell phones, for example, or dirty diamond exports from West Africa on our fingers, or dirty coal taken from Appalachia through mountaintop removal).

Third, through a whole range of complex and newly invented financial instruments, a rich minority has succeeded in profiting from our retirement accounts and investments and real estate values.

Fourth, through skyrocketing debt, we keep trying to prop up both our personal and national wealth … purchasing our own prosperity on the backs of future generations who will have to pay the mortgage.

How can we create a new kind of economy that heals rather than destroys creation, that takes into account the needs and dreams of the poor majority in

> *our world and not just the super-rich minority, that diverts funds from swords*
> *and spears to plowshares and pruning hooks?*

The conversation in this book also grows from other economic conversations at the global level. Economics begins in seeking answers to the curse of poverty and the creation of wealth. My own experience in forming *slum-dwellers' theologies* has involved a constant search to answer two pressing questions faced by two billion slum-dwellers globally as to how the poor of the slums escape poverty, and how to break oppressive barriers that lock them there.

These complex issues are the field of economists. But many economists would say, "Surely it is not the realm of theology? We deal with the material; you deal with the spiritual."

While the discipline of economics has been demonstrated historically to be limited to a certain subset of issues and often unable to relate these to social realities,. While it has historically relegated Christianity only to the spiritual, economic issues are central to the unfolding Biblical narrative.   Thus Christians have a much wider understanding of the holism of engagement with the physical world that includes economics as a subset, and hence we must voice that holism, even if economists would possibly reject that voice though most are people of reason. The covenants of the scriptures are defined in terms of God-man-land paradigms. The gospel itself is rooted in economic theology as we shall see.

Ten Principles Healthy Kiwi Economics

Having critiqued reductionism in economics I myself will be guilty of the same in this book, but I suspect you will agree that this is done justifiably and not in a damaging way. In multiple teaching contexts, both in the first world and with slum pastors, I have tried to reduce such a theology into some manageable pattern and hence have developed a pattern of teaching the fifty(?) or is it a hundred(?) Biblical principles around ten core themes (see diagram at the start of the book).

New Zealand Christians have been significant figures in the building of our national economic systems across the decades, and have fostered major economic themes of the Scriptures. The first of these is *love or respect for human dignity* (1), of humans being created in the image of God. An image which we must neither scar nor mar.

This Christian principle is foundational to an innovative society full of *creativity* (2), *productivity* (3) (a theme only Christianity as a religion affirms, and *cooperative economics* (4) that underlie much that is healthy in New Zealand's economic growth and the national fight to sustain both *work and rest* (5). These are paralleled by ministries from many churches to sectors of poor in the community, including almost every church in Auckland – the beautiful servant bride of Christ - reaching out to migrants. These represent the search to apply other biblical principles of *equity and redistribution* (7). Underlying all, has been a dramatic drama of establishing a nation where *ownership* of land (9) by all was (though no longer is) feasible.

A good friend commented on reasons he migrated to New Zealand mentioning that our New Zealand economy is in reasonable health by many measures; the country has sought to create a harmonious society, the envy of the world; there is relative equality; a social welfare safety net that works well; our democracy works reasonably well; with a government that is fair, balanced and doing a good job managing the economy. The nation has been by international standards, reasonably well *managed* (8), despite the multiple follies of our leaders.

Yet in the last decades there are major arenas where the Biblical mandate has been violated. It is apparent on returning to New Zealand after a decade, that governments, year by year, have increased the levels of pressure on New Zealanders to produce. This has positively included the increase of productivity and employment. Negatively it includes deliberate policies to "force" women into the workforce (very different to providing choices) in order to increase productivity;[4] increases of the tax take over the 90's;[5] attempts at destruction of the power of the trade unions and collective bargaining processes (developed to protect the poorest workers); the creation of an indebted student population and the selling of the crown jewels - land, banking, forestry, infrastructure assets to foreign interests in the name of encouraging investment; a decrease in equality - to name some. Greed, the opposite of the principle of *simplicity* (6) has become glorified with multi-millionaires earning notoriety, and even becoming prime minister.

The reassertion of *freedom* (10) and *human dignity* (1) against such policies is crucial for the sustaining of a *just and good society*. While there is much evidence of Christians bringing Biblical principles into the national legislative process, the reflections in these chapters each indicate ongoing potential applications into the workplace of the value, the worth, the creativity, of the dignity of each individual. This is part of the historic warfare of the church against the world, the historic process of Christians rebelling against exploitation, oppression, inequality and injustice.

Principles of Detachment in a Consumer Society

In a context of increasing differentials between rich and poor and forced expansion of indebtedness via credit card, postmodern discipleship cannot be less than economic, if it is to be true to Jesus' words. He asks us for *detachment, separation and rejection of the values of the world* (6). For example, following Jesus' simple statement that, *the cares of the world, the delight in riches and the desire for other things enter in and choke the Word,*[6] classic Christian discipleship has developed principles of *simplicity and detachment* in its rejection of greed, the accumulation of wealth and consumerism.

While for some decades, post-World War II, we enjoyed the expansion of wealth, the abolition of poverty and the freedom of the middle class, now global Capitalism has morphed into what Jane Kelsey defines as the FIRE (Finances, Insurance, Real Estate) economy, and we now are paying a price for the violation of other biblical principles of *stewardship* (8), and *remaining debt-free* (8) and wealth for godly *work* (5) (vs. creation of paper money and usury). One of those costs is the increasing debt burden on New Zealanders.

The underlying principle beneath the success of Capitalism and *production* (2) or wealth creation, is accessible and easily legalised acquisition of *land for housing* (10). With security of *ownership* through a just legal system, capital developments can be made on that *land*. In New Zealand that is usually the basis of obtaining capital for small business development. The FIRE economy has likely destroyed that option for our children.

Conversation Gap Between God and Economies

While the principles are simple, our postmodern world is increasingly complex. The latter half of this book reflects on economic systems developed over the last two centuries far removed from those of the previous millennia.

The great transition away from this standard of *detachment* occurred with the failure of the puritans after Calvin (from the late 1600's onwards), to keep ethical regimentation on *profitable industry*. As Britain led the world into the new consumer and technological age, Archbishop William Temple (1881-1942) indicates that the church for 150 years (now 250), failed to sustain a consistent public critique of these sins. Christian Socialism and "the social gospel" - an attempt in the early 1900's to develop Christ's teachings into a moral framework for Christendom - spoke to *redistribution of wealth* (7), and dealt with the popular value systems of ordinary Christians in their call to the principles of *co-operative economics* (4). It did not involve a call to *simplicity without greed* (6), in the midst of increasingly competitive systems.[7]

This directly contrasts with earlier Calvinism, with its understanding of the just *work* (4) that uses resources for the common good, frugality, diligence and their relationship to the emergence of Capitalism.[8]

The churches subsequently have mostly failed to reflect significantly on these systems. There are exceptions: Abraham Kuyper (1837 -1920),[9] the Dutch theologian-politician, reflected on these issues using a *theology of spheres of action* – the political, economic, educational, etc; Martin Hengel, a German theologian in *Property and Riches in the Early Church*,[10] did a superb process of exegeting economics in the scriptures; *liberation theologians* have taken up Marxist categories and sought to Christianise them;[11] as does Michael Novak for American Capitalism in *The Spirit of Democratic Capitalism* - reflections propagated through Acton Institute gatherings. Novak's statement rings true:

> *In no major sphere of life have the traditions of theology fallen further behind. For many centuries, of course, there was no science of economics and no sustained economic growth. So the lack was hardly felt. Today it is a scandal.*[12]

Discipling Nations

The command is that we disciple the nation, bringing not just individuals but its peoples and cultures and structures to follow Kingdom principles.

From a simple study of the Kingdom of God as it impinges on economics, we can lay the framework from which to build conversations in New Zealand with the issues of our day. Because economics is so complex that even economists disagree, we tend to leave these things to the experts and the secular politicians. But the command is that we disciple the nation, bringing not just individuals but its peoples and cultures and structures in line with Kingdom principles, so we must engage. That can begin simply with common people applying some simple Biblical principles.

2. The Genesis of Economics

or The Economics of Genesis

In this chapter, we examine the foundations of economics found in the nature of God revealed in Genesis chapter 1,[1] and expanded through the Pentateuch (the first five books of the Bible, ascribed to Moses). We understand that Moses heard from God but understood God's directives in terms of an eclectic set of anthropological sources as an Egyptian General, a desert wanderer, and son of Jewish slaves. Genesis gives the history of a tribal society, which then in the slavery of Egypt encounters the depravity of urban poverty. In reaction, Moses utilises his wealth of knowledge of societal structures from Ethiopia, Egypt and Midian to create the political economic framework of a mixed urban-tribal society in the promised land.

Hermeneutics are important. We cannot just take quotations from an ancient tribal context, or an emerging agrarian society and apply them willy-nilly to post-modern society. Rather we can examine the principles of God's actions in redemptive history, and their consistency over multiple interventions over the ages. The question for later in the book then becomes how to interpret those principles into 20th century con-urbanisations.

King of Creation

In the beginning, God... When we speak of God's creation it is important to remember that God created all things.[2] He rules and reigns the universe from before the beginning! He is King of Creation! When we speak of the Kingdom of God we speak of *God's active, interventive rule redeeming humanity and restoring the creation.* This has always existed and always will. The coming of the Kingdom of God in the New Testament is a breaking in of that Kingdom into the human condition. It is a redemption of those things that were once in bondage to other than what God created them to be.

God is the first creator. He is the first worker and provider. He does not hoard the economic resources. He creates people to share in the fruits of his creation. God is the example of sharing and of what our creations should be used for.

The first thing that God does with his creation is sit back and reflect on it. God sees that *it is good.* He is the source of this creation and he must take pleasure that what he has done is good. Secondly God creates things *for the benefit of others.* God creates the animals and Eve so that Adam will not be alone. These are the two elements that must be part of all work, production and creation - that it pleases God and that it serves humanity.

The Nature of Land & Technology

Things were made good by God from the very beginning and they were seen as good. The land, the waters, the animals, humans were all created as good and in a pleasant garden. Work was a gift of expression and creativity not a burden. It was not until after the fall when humans sinned, that the earth was cursed. It was not until after the fall that work became a burden.

After the fall, however, many of these things were cursed: birth, marriage, the ground, plants, work, products[3]. More importantly than the cursing of resources and earthly relationships was the enmity and distance created between humanity and God. Without this basic central guideline, humanity lost much of its ability to use resources for good. That is, without the relationship with God and a *blessed relationship* with each other, humanity could not use the resources that God gave them for their purpose. This purpose was to please God and to serve the good of our neighbour.

Without this natural relationship that was in the Garden, God had to impose an unnatural one. Not one that is a free-flowing expression of who people are, but instead one that is imposed. This took the form of Law. The law should be held in high regard considering its source, but it is not the first intention of God. The Law was instituted because our human nature designed to please God and love our neighbour was damaged. These were now things that needed to be followed in obedience. But this did not always happen.

Many times throughout Israel's history there were abuses of God's creation. Their possessions may come to rule them, so God told them, "Beware."

> Work + Obedience = Blessing & Wealth
>
> Work - Obedience = Curse & Poverty

Economic success may also cause them to be proud and forget God.[4]

Many wisely use and manage these resources, but it is God who makes them *fruitful*. Leviticus 26 is a beautiful chapter showing the interrelationship of people's work and God's blessing on a nation.

The Wisdom Literature tells us that things are an unstable basis on which to build life since they will all vanish away.[5] The wisest man tells us that as a goal in life, they are an illusion.[6] Those who depend on them will fall like autumn leaves.[7] These point to some of the dangers of riches. They could be good things, but only if they are put to the use that God intended.

As resources have morphed into modern day technological products, most of these derivative products are good and serve the common good. But this new technology is going to disrupt the old, and we need to move with the times, for it is God who gave us the capacity to create such technologies off his creation. Thus a godly nation will have a rapidly evolving and technologically responsive, creative cultural environment.

Land

The land was created by God and was created good. Our job as humans in the garden was to *till and care* for the land. Too often, the emphasis has been on the "subduing and dominion" over the creation of God. Humanity both before and after the curse was to work the land and *manage and care* for it. Land was seen as a way of providing for the family. The land is God's and must be treated as such. It must be nurtured and taken care of. The land will produce abundance if God's people are faithful to the care of it and to the covenant established between them and *Yahweh*. If they are not faithful, then the land would be barren.[8]

The land was created by God and is God's. It is not to be owned in perpetuity by any individual.[9]. Therefore wanton abuse of it and poor stewardship of the land will result in God's curse instead of his blessing.[10]

God is the one who gives his people the ability to obtain wealth and he is the one who takes it away. These resources are taken away with idolatry and oppression.[11] These bring a curse on the land.

The Role of Dusty Humanity

Humans were made from the dust of the earth.[12] They were created to subdue and bring it into subjection, to rule the life in the earth, the sky and the sea.[13] It is delegated authority. They are to rule as the image of God,[14] in a caring way of tilling and keeping. This creation mandate is not an excuse for an ecological crisis.

The way that God ruled was to give every living thing that he created away. Every plant and animal was given away for the provision of humanity. If this is the image in which we were created, then we also must have the same attitude when it comes to our resources. They must be given away for the provision of others, not so they may simply eat off our production, but so they also may produce off the resources we have created.

Therefore our role is to both create resources to be given away and to produce things that will be pleasing to God. If we are producing resources for our own gain or that will be displeasing to God's reflection, then we are not existing in the way in which we were created, and not being children of the Kingdom of God. This is the way of godly economics, the way of love.

Prosperity & Wealth Creation

The managing of the earth so it is *productive* (2), is a foundational principle. To work hard in the tilling of the soil, brings an increase on average of perhaps 3% per year. On this productivity, societies could be built. There are others mentioned in the Genesis narrative who became specialists, artisans, indicating the transition from a tribal form of society to one where there is enough excess income to support such specialists.

Wealth in the Old Testament was usually attributed to righteousness within the tribe. Beginning with Abraham, when the people were obedient to God's commandments then they prospered. Amos warned God's people that they must obey his commands or the Northern Kingdom would be destroyed. The people did not obey and God followed through on his promise.[15] Wealth and riches are two aspects of the world's resources that it is our responsibility to manage - all resources which must be used to please God and serve humanity.

Prosperity is the result of the Lord's blessings.

> *You crown the year with bounty*
> *And your carts overflow with abundance.*
> *The grasslands of the wilderness overflow*
> *...they shout for joy and sing.*[16]

God blessed Abraham because of his faith. He blessed him because of his tithe to Melchizadech, the priest of Salem.

God's prosperity and blessing is not the same as the Pentecostal TV evangelist's *prosperity gospel*, which is a form of manipulation and magic. It says, "if you give your tithe *to me, God's anointed*, God will bless you". That is manipulation for personal gain, not dissimilar to the old Catholic practice of buying one's way to heaven. Magic is when one makes a relationship between one thing being the cause of another. It makes logical links that are not valid or truthful. First, that because someone (the TV preacher) has money or crowds, they are successful and blessed. Secondly, that there is a magical relationship between giving and blessing. Jesus taught that the widow's mite was blessed because of her heart. The rich man gave but was not blessed. The formula is not universal. It is relational. Thirdly, that giving aside from following other financial principles is all that one must do to experience God's blessings. We need to apply all ten of these Biblical principles to see prosperity! We need to be obedient to all his teaching! This is little different to the magic many lived under before they were converted!

The Poor

One fundamental questions of economics, is the question of how we establish systems that lift people out of poverty. To answer this "the poor" is a term requiring definition and responses to poverty evaluated. In doing so, it is not intended to place people in a derogatory box. Usually, in my conferences training urban poor pastors, the question they most want answers to is how the city causes them to live in such poverty. This is a significant theme throughout the scriptures.

In *Companion to the Poor,*[17] I classify eight Hebrew and Greek words into three categories of poverty and examine Biblical responses.

- Those poor through *calamity* and no fault of their own, including the widows, orphans, lame, blind, deaf, frail, elderly: For these the Kingdom of God seeks to alleviate their suffering, the church constantly is involved in supporting the widows and orphans, we are to give to everyone who has need, and uplift these poor.
- Those poor through *their own sins* - such as gambling, drunkenness, miserliness, sleeping too much, poor planning... The response of the Kingdom is to preach the gospel and call for repentance, so that the Spirit of God may set people free.
- Those poor through *oppression and dispossession*, the sins of others against them: In these contexts of injustice, the gospel seeks to bring justice. In contexts of dispossession, the gospel seeks to restore land rights. In contexts of oppression, the gospel speaks against the oppressors. And in all of this we look to a God who rules over those with power and will one day judge them severely. These oppressed poor become the godly poor in the scriptures, those who turn to God in the midst of their pain.

It is clear from this word study that most of the poor were not poor through sinful activities. The prophets described the Messiah as one of the oppressed poor and those for whom the Messiah would come were the oppressed. Jesus quotes these prophets in his *blessed are the poor in Spirit, for theirs is the Kingdom.* The blessing is not in poverty but in the Kingdom which sets people free from the effects of calamity, from personal sins, from oppressive systems.

Interest and Loans for the Poor

Exodus 22:25-27 is part of laws that seek to regulate the treatment and protect the interests of disenfranchised and vulnerable groups within Israel.[18] Subsistence loans, as well as compassionate handling of essential items such as pawning clothes, were meant to help people cope with extreme poverty so they not be a source of gain for the lenders. We are to be supportive and compassionate, treating such people with the kindness that they would show to resident aliens. Solidarity is to be expressed by refraining from the charging of interest.

The sabbatical laws of Deuteronomy 15:1–18 aims to alleviate suffering caused by debt and oppression among the Israelite community. Borrowing was and is integral to people needing support. But the sabbatical principle is here applied to the matter of debt, commanding creditors to remit their claims every seven years—saying *no* to the economic system that ties people inexorably in debt. The passage contains the stark statement, *There should be no poor among you* (v.4), contrasted with, *There will always be poor people among you* (v 11). This seeming contradiction sets the agenda: the reality of a fallen world is that poverty persists, but the ultimate intention of God is that it should be abolished.

Deut 23:19–20 explicitly forbids the charging of interest within the Israelite community while permitting interest on loans to foreigners. In the former case, the prohibition is spelt out as applying to *interest on money, interest on provisions, or interest on anything that is lent*. It is not confined simply to poor Israelites. Obedience to this command is linked to God's blessing: *so that the Lord your God may bless you in all your undertakings*. The close-knit community ties that lie at the heart of the prohibition are highlighted by the permission to treat foreigners differently. This was not the stranger living in their midst, but the stranger who lived in a foreign nation, with whom there was no land-kinship network. In that context, levying interest on loans represented a sensible minimisation of risk, and meant that Israel could take its place as an equal partner in the commercial arena of the ancient Middle East.

There are other Old Testament texts that mention interest more briefly, but always with a mark of disapproval. In Israel, it was among the defining marks of righteousness that a person did not lend at interest. The person who may dwell in God's sanctuary is one *who lends his money without interest,*[19] and the righteous man of Ezekiel[20] is similarly defined. Nehemiah becomes very angry when he learns of Israelites exacting interest from their fellow-countrymen and forcing them into financial slavery.[21]

The morphing of these principles into the 21st Century will be discussed in later chapters.

Living on Quail and Manna

Beyond the natural laws of wealth creation and financial stewardship that God has put in place, there are mysterious elements of spirituality, of God's blessings above and beyond on those who trust in him.

There is a consistent theme of God's blessing on the righteous. As they go about their normal business, he adds more to it. In the story of Abraham, and then of Jacob,[22] we see particular blessing because of (imperfect) faith, righteousness and promise.

If God is your source, then why are you struggling to make ends meet? He's *Jehovah Jireh*, your Provider.[23] The world is full of solutions like focusing on your wants. God's solution is very different. He says to focus on Him and then everything else will follow. He has a plan for you, and He wants you to follow His strategy.

The provision of manna and quail as they wandered in the Sinai desert for forty years after being saved from Egypt,[24] gives an additional theme. In this case, the provision is far beyond a simple blessing of normal life processes. God creates exceptional processes, beyond the normal, to feed the poor, wandering, emergent nation, despite their disobedience. He does this because of a covenant relationship. It is not something others can presume upon.

In the story of Elijah, we find this same supernatural provision, where for three years of famine, ravens brought him bread and meat in the morning and the evening.[25] This supernatural provision continued for Elijah as he stayed with the widow of Zarephath. Each day as the widow cooked, the Lord replenished the supply of flour and oil.

Redistribution: The Tithe

Each community of faith throughout history has some structured process to ensure the flow of wealth for the priests, the preachers, the apostles, or the prophets.

The dedication of a tenth to God was recognised as a duty before the time of Moses. Abraham paid tithes to Melchizedek);[26] and Jacob vowed to the Lord and said, *Of all that you will give me I will surely give the tenth to you.*

Every Jew was required by the Levitical law to pay three tithes of his property: (1) one tithe for the Levites; (2) one for the use of the temple and the great feasts and (3) one for the poor of the land.

The first Mosaic law on this subject is recorded in Leviticus 27:30-32. Subsequent legislation regulated the destination of the tithes. The paying of the tithes was an important part of the Jewish religious worship. In the days of Hezekiah one of the first results of the reformation of religion was the eagerness with which the people brought in their tithes.[27] The neglect of this duty was sternly rebuked by the prophets.[28]

In many ways the symbolic integration of all these principles is in the institution of the Jubilee, and ancient Ethiopian custom from before the time of Moses, that he converted for the building of a national consensus regarding equity.

3. Jubilee Justice

How do these Old Testament principles connect to the New Testament? A key to answer that, is in the content of Jesus' Gospel? When people heard him preach *The Spirit of the Lord is upon me, because he has anointed me to preach good news to the poor* ,[1] what did they understand?

They heard him declare an eternal Jubilee of liberty from oppression for he was quoting from the Servant Songs of Isaiah, four songs that prophesied the nature of the coming Messiah and his bringing justice to the earth.[2]

So what was this Jubilee that we began to explore in the previous chapter as we reflected on the Biblical theology of economics in the Pentateuch? As a political economic structure we are wise to examine its context, its specifics and then find the dynamic equivalents in today's society. We cannot simply take the specifics and impose them on another culture in another millennium.

Background: Genesis of Work and Rest

> In the fall, humanity went from fulfilment to frustration; from gardener to farmer.

The Jubilee is primarily a time of rest, so is built on the nature of God expressed in the first chapters of Genesis. God is the first worker and the first rester. When God created he also rested, because he rested, the task he was doing must be seen as work. Yet for God this was not toil by any means, but a way to create and express beauty. By resting and reflecting again and again that *it is good,* God shows us the example of both what work should be and what rest should be. He rested not out of exhaustion but out of completion and in order to enjoy the work of his hands.

God's work was creative; making something from nothing; out of chaos creating order; through naming he brings into being; His work is artistic. All of these are godly functions of godly work in which we can reflect his image.

His work can be broken down into four different categories: creation, providence, judgment, redemption. These are the tasks of God. Christian theology of vocation has developed these extensively. Alistair McKenzie of Christchurch[3] has applied these historic teachings to the 21st Century Kiwi context.

Work was created before the fall and is therefore to be seen as good. Work had received a bad reputation from other cultures whose god's felt that work was beneath them and created humanity to do the work. In the Hebrew tradition work has much honour and can be seen as a holy commandment from God. To till and keep the land is an honourable and holy role.

After the fall, work was cursed by God. This did not change the fact that it was still a duty commanded by God. The difference now was that work was toil instead of the creative process that it was originally intended to be. Humanity went from fulfilment to frustration; from gardener to farmer. Throughout the Bible, work still contains its dignity: David as a shepherd, Saul the farmer. There was no shame in common work.

Even though there was this high esteem for work there was still the view that work could be and was abused. This took two forms: idleness and overwork. Idleness is condemned in the Wisdom literature.[4] It is seen as the path of the wicked. But

> **The Sabbath**
> Re-creation
> of the soil,
> of the soul,
> of the society!

overwork based on ambition, was also condemned as folly in the book of Ecclesiastes. The reminder to not overwork is in the teaching on the Sabbath.

The Sabbath

Work without rest was one of the major sins warned about by God. The Sabbath[5] was instituted, not only as a symbol of the covenant between God and his people but it was also a time to reflect and rest. The Sabbath was established by God as a day of rest. Rest is a time of reflection on the week. It is out of this reflection that worship is naturally brought out and later established. Rest must include worship. God's rest was a reflection on his work and seeing that it was good. Our rest is a reflection on God's provision and his work, as it is combined with our work and obedience. It results in worshipping God because it is all good.

God's overall plan is that there is an established pattern between work and rest. Neither are complete by themselves. There is good in rest and refreshment and in production and work. The two are the natural fruit of obedience to and worship of God.

4000 Year Old Tribal Customs in Northern Kenya

Two of the major festivals of Israel in the scriptures were the year of Jubilee and the Sabbath year. The Sabbath was to be an ecological, a societal, and an economic rest period. It was to be a time to allow for the recreation of the soil, of the soul and of the society. It was to be a time to remember that it is the Lord who provides - that same Lord who provided manna in the wilderness.

31

But they frequently violated the Sabbath. The Sabbath was so important that the Lord exiled the Jews for seventy years, enough to make up for the Sabbaths that had not been kept.

> I was speaking in Kenya at a conference on Land Rights. I sat in front of an older English gentleman. As we talked, I discovered he had led the Kenyan National Council of Churches, having lived in Kenya for forty years. He told me a story about the Jubilee.
>
> On a trip near the Ethiopian border he had spent time with a tribe that since before the time of Moses had celebrated the Jubilee as part of the economic structure of their people. While God spoke to Moses, he did not speak in a vacuum. And in applying the principles of the Jubilee to our urban context, we also do not do so in a vacuum.

The Jubilee

The Jubilee,[6] seven times seven years or every 50th year, took these values a step further, redistributing the sources of wealth, the means of production of the society. It was a time of equalizing.

It is synonymous with the year of liberty. Slaves are to be set free. Freedom is inherent in the gospel message.

The year of Jubilee was the great re-distributor of the land for the people of Israel. Every fifty years, the land must be returned to the original tribes, clans and families to whom God had given it. It is these tribes that see that the land is distributed justly and nurtured in such a way as to bear fruit. If the land is sold it is only for the period of time remaining until the year of Jubilee. All debts were cancelled, all obligations were nullified. It was the time of celebration. A day when all could have the same start with the same resources. Thus, redistribution of the means of production is inherent in the gospel message. Debts are to be cancelled. Economic freedom is inherent in the gospel message. Celebration is inherent in the gospel message.

Urban lands - dwelling places inside of a walled city - were excluded from this redistribution, for the value of urban land had nothing to do with agricultural production. The year of Jubilee only pertains to those resources that have a way of producing sustenance and livelihood, not to the individual's home. So urban land could be bought and sold.

That did not foresee the era of urban land speculation of the modern megacity. There are some who would identify the development of small business as the equivalent of urban land, for it is these that enables much productivity in our society - this idea has merit.

On the other hand, home ownership is foundational to building capital for investment in small business, and the constant increase in speculation of land prices in the city violates the core concepts of the Jubilee. Urban land and farm land today both largely gain value from increase in value of the land not the produce of the land. So there is not a need for the same differentiation.

One way to insure that people were not subjected to generational poverty and eventually oppression was this Year of Jubilee. By celebrating this, the people of Israel insured that the resources that God had provided were evenly distributed. Distinction between classes of people could not exist when the commandment of the year of Jubilee was followed. When Israel failed to implement the Jubilee, the wealth was established amongst the few and oppression of those without expanded. Thus the prophets rail against the rich, and defend the oppressed poor in stratified Israel.

Basis of Production

There are some who would identify the development of small business in the city as the equivalent of rural land in the Jubilee, for these are the basis of productivity in our society.

Redistribution in New Zealand includes a very effective welfare system, the gradated tax system, and philanthropy enshrined in historic Charitable Trust laws and modelled by a number of leading businessmen. Some would argue for an estate tax on the wealthy (In the US, is it is a tax on an estate worth more than $250,000). In many ways these have implemented some of what the Jubilee was attempting.

Figure 3: The cross profoundly turns economics on its head.

4. Economic Jesus

The day we meet and fall in love with Jesus Christ, the Lord of life, of creation, of wealth, our values are totally changed, just as Zacheus' values were drastically reoriented by his confrontation with Jesus.[1] Discipleship begins with an all-consuming love and allegiance to Jesus Christ - an undivided, single-minded love for him. And he is the one who has absolute rights of ownership over us and our possessions.

Discipleship is a pilgrimage of obedience,[2] a daily process of learning how to do his commands,[3] and this involves bringing all decisions about work, about property, about bank-balances into conformity with his commands. This book is to enable us more deeply to love Him as we learn to obey Him in this area of finances and possessions.[4]

One verse in four in Jesus' teaching talks of issues related to economics. We can only skim briefly over the topic. We will start by exploring the source of those thoughts in the development of the Old Testament. Every philosophic theme in the Bible begins in the first chapters of Genesis, so we need to contrast Jesus teaching with these themes and look at the continuities and the discontinuities.

The Kingdom of God

The King has Come

What differentiates the New Testament from the Old? The difference is found in a small baby in a little manger in an insignificant town surrounded by a host of angels, shepherds and wise men. The King has come! The Kingdom of God has invaded the Kingdom of the ruler of this world. The Kingdom is now in the midst of us.[5]

In the Old Testament the king intervened periodically in the life of Israel. Now he has invaded! Immanuel, God with us! 2000 years ago he stepped out of riches, out of honour - the one whose finger placed the stars, the Word who created the heavens, stepped out of his court into the poverty of a manger, from the choirs of heaven into the silence of a carpenters shop, where no rays of glory shone.[6]

That incarnation was the most profound economic decision since creation. It shook and shakes the very structures of world economics and one day will result in total and absolute eternal demise of all economies. That incarnation was one act in God's redemptive history, a history of redemption among the poor and oppressed in the earth, for the world's economics are the economics of oppression, incarnation economics are those of the oppressed. The incarnate Kingdom of God redeems the resources that God has given to us.

The two commandments given by the herald of the Kingdom are: *you shall love the Lord your God with all your heart, soul ,mind, and strength, and you shall love your neighbour as yourself.* All that we are and all that we have must be put forth to please God and serve humanity. This is God's first economic principle and it is the greatest commandment of Jesus.

Jesus came preaching *The Kingdom of Heaven is at hand, repent and believe the gospel.*[7] He came living it, ruling over creation - both as man, working as a carpenter for 30 years - and as God, for as he went about preaching he *went about doing good and healing all who were oppressed by the devil.*[8] That healing is also healing for the pains of our poverty.

He not only preached the presence of the Kingdom, he demonstrated that Satan's work were destroyed.[9] When the disciples came back enthusiastic because even the demons were subject to them he tells them *I saw Satan fall like lighting from Heaven.*[10] Finally he triumphed over Satan in death. Satan was rendered inoperative.[11]

> **Incarnation as Economic Disruption**
>
> The incarnation was the most profound economic act since creation. It shook the very structures of world economics and one day will result in total demise of all economies in the revelation of a totally new ecological and technological earth.

The Kingdom Will Come

Yet the teaching of the scriptures is that the Kingdom is still to come.[12] Jesus came the first time, humbly, quietly as foretold in the servant psalms,[13] not as judge but as saviour.[14] He brought his Kingdom into the world. One day he will return again, to *break the Kingdoms of this world*[15] and establish the rule of the Kingdom forever.

So we are in an in-between stage, we enjoy a taste of its blessings here now. *We have tasted of the powers of the age to come,*[16] through the Holy Spirit who lives within us as *our seal,* our signature on a contract affirming our future.[17] Through his power, we experience a foretaste of future blessings. At times he restores our bodies through healings, though usually we have to wait for his coming when we will receive new bodies.[18] He gives us power over the evil one by his Spirit,[19] but Satan is not yet cast into the place prepared for him.[20] At times we see clearly, as the Spirit of Truth guides us,[21] but mostly *we see in a mirror, darkly.* On that day when all are resurrected, *we will see clearly.*[22]

The New Created Order

Jesus, the herald of the Kingdom of God, not only redeems humanity, but also creation within it. The Kingdom of God is here now, so we can now retrieve the way things were created in the Garden. We no longer have to follow the guidelines of the Law of the Old Testament (though it is part of our new nature to do so), instead we can be transformed into new creations who know what the will of God is - to do that which is good, acceptable, and perfect;[23] to work and *manage resources(8)* to please God; to use them to *love humanity(1)*; to bring all of the environment out of its bondage and *set it free(10)*.[24]

The way that the created order can be reinstated to God's original purpose depends upon the proclamation of the Good News.[25] The Kingdom of God is here yet not fully realised. Until it is fully realised there will exist two different Kingdoms. One is a Kingdom of the Spirit... for *the Kingdom of God is not a matter of eating and drinking but of righteousness, peace and joy in the Holy Spirit...*[26] yet a Kingdom that profoundly transforms economics.

> *If you lend to those from whom you hope to receive, what good is that to you? For even sinners do the same... But love your enemies, do good, and lend, expecting nothing in return.*[27]

The other, the Kingdom of this world is symbolised through the scriptures and in their great climax[28] as *Babylon*, a great religious-political economic conglomerate that has grown out of the rebellion of humanity - its very nature is that of oppression, exploitation and unrighteousness. It is at heart a massive worldwide market place,[29] eventually dominated by a single authority[30] (for in the scriptures unrighteousness is far more related to the abuse of power than the struggles for survival of the poor) in the midst of an increasingly lawless world.

Both Kingdoms are constantly in battle with each other. We are promised that the Kingdom of God will eventually be brought in fully with the return of Christ.

New Economic Role for Humanity

One of our main economic roles is found in proclaiming the Kingdom of God, both in word and deed.[31] Proclamation is particularly among the poor,[32] for whom it is a message of mercy, but not neglecting others. For it is to bring all people in every nation, all of their peoples, classes society and culture into obedience to him.[33]

Battle has been engaged (a spiritual engagement for the souls of mankind, not a *jihad* war).[34] Many will die for siding with the King. Todd Johnson estimates one hundred and sixty thousand martyrs per year are martyred for their faith.[35] He has come destroying the works of Satan and calls us to be his ambassadors.[36]

This role of proclamation as the central activity in the battle will cut across family relationships like a sword,[37] an apparent denial of being our brothers' keeper. It will be costly in terms of personal success, but we have to sit down and count the cost of whether we can afford not to be involved with the King.[38] It further requires those who preach to a *forsaking of possessions* (6),[39] an apparent denial of the Old Testament mandate to spend our time in managing the earth.

> *As they were going along the road, a man said to him, Lord, I will follow you wherever you may go. Jesus replied, "Foxes have holes and birds of the air have nests, but the son of man has nowhere to lay his head."*[40]

Jesus himself chose to have few possessions, no place to lay his head. He taught his disciples this pattern of economics. In Acts we find them discipling others in the same lifestyle.[41] He promises that *renunciation of possessions* (6) will find recognition with God.[42] He tells us not to worry about daily needs,[43] and refused to arbitrate a land dispute. In Acts, we find the disciples of the disciples selling their possessions, their own houses and lands, so the teaching multiplied at the foundation of the early church.[44]

But lest we overemphasise Jesus' poverty, let us also note that he grew up with a carpentry business, and was well supported by well-to-do women.[45] He tells us to use possessions to support our parents and those in need.[46] He was not an ascetic. Nor a beggar. God provided his needs, and he provided for other's needs.

Jesus laid no universal demand for poverty on people. His concern was with our financial status in terms of our total commitments to the cause of proclaiming the Kingdom. Chosen poverty itself has no virtue (though St Francis of Assisi believed it did)! The issue here is total commitment to the call of Jesus, and the need to proclaim the Kingdom.

For Jesus chose an apostolic lifestyle. And Paul chose an apostolic missionary lifestyle. We find Paul, thirty years later, preaching the Kingdom of God and teaching about the Lord Jesus while a prisoner in Rome.[47] For the sake of this proclamation he became *all things to all people*.[48] He was *as poor, yet making many rich; as having nothing, yet possessing everything*.[49] Coming from a rich family, he knew how to enjoy good things. However, he had learned for the sake of the gospel, *how to be abased and how to abound*.[50] He followed what Jesus taught his disciples that though all other normal functions of a healthy life are good and permissible, they are no longer the priority.[51]

39

Jesus' Message of the Jubilee

The theme of the Jubilee becomes central to the New Testament, and as such, central to our understanding of the nature of the gospel. In the central passage around which Luke builds his gospel and the Acts, Luke 4:18, Jesus declares his mission and as he does so, he inaugurates the Jubilee eternally.

Here Jesus declares his commission and ours, his gospel and ours. It was to be good news for the poor? But what could be good news to the poor? What is the master talking about? What is the content of the gospel?

He describes it as a proclamation of freedom, as a release from oppression, as the coming of a special year. What do these phrases mean? These are allusions and references to the Old Testament idea of the year of Jubilee. He is declaring that the Jubilee has come - forever. The rest from oppression, slavery is here, forever.

The scroll he had been given in this little synagogue in the little Jewish enclave of Nazareth (amid so many foreign villages), contained a passage in Isaiah 61:1 - one of the servant songs, four prophecies about the coming Messiah.[52] He speaks of the year of the Lord's favour. The Jews had been exiled because of their disobedience about this year. For seventy years the land was left fallow to recover from four hundred and ninety years of use without rest. And their expectation was that when they returned, the land would again be blessed by God.

But the expectation was not fulfilled and four hundred years of silence from God settled on the land as they awaited a Messiah. So when Jesus quotes this verse he is saying he is the Messiah, the one who brings the Jubilee.

Isa 49:8 calls this year, the time of my favour, the day of my salvation. This day would be a day of covenant, this day would be a day of restoration of the land. This day will be a day when captives, slaves, oppressed people will find their chains fall off. Paul tells us, *now is the acceptable time, now is the time of my favour.*[53] We live in the now of the Jubilee. This is good news for the poor.

Howard Snyder does an excellent theological analysis of the Jubilee, from multiple theological sources,

> *Jesus does not seem to have been inaugurating a Jubilee year. Rather he was announcing the Jubilee age – the very kingdom of God (Matt 4:17)…Jesus' literal, historical healings, like his resurrection, are signs of the literal, historical character and in-breaking of the new order of God's Kingdom.*[54]

A Liberating Gospel

The command to blow the trumpet to announce the Jubilee age has never ceased. Wherever we declare this good news we create the *chaos of liberation, and with liberty comes celebration* (10). Whenever people experience conversion, and the entrance of the Holy Spirit into their lives we find this great release of joy, this immersion in the Holy Spirit can be uncontainable. Whenever Jesus healed or delivered, whenever Pentecostal brothers and sisters heal or deliver, there is unending joy.

This is also the reality of the bride of Christ, the historic church. When I was setting up our first Protestant missionary apostolic order in New Zealand, I remember tracking down a rotund Anglican Franciscan Friar. He was the epitome of what we consider St Francis, always joking, enjoying life in the midst of chosen poverty. To be set free from slavery is surely to become a celebrating, worshipping, joy-filled person. The Jewish calendar had three and then four holidays where people were to celebrate. In a schizophrenic post-modern society epitomised by Madonna, how desperate is the need of true celebration. And indeed the Sunday worship and feasting of our four thousand churches reverberates weekly through our communities in New Zealand.

And when those, who are more staid, bring these principles of liberation into the structures of society, the groans of the people also are transformed into celebration.

Does this mean we are to espouse Liberation Theology? That theology is different to the liberty, to the freedom that Jesus talks of here. But it has its roots in these passages. It builds from both Marxism and Jesus, so when we work alongside those trained in its thinking, we find ourselves aligning with the values of those who would incarnate among the poor and seek justice through people movements and structural reform, and at the same time we find ourselves rejecting the bitterness and social analysis of the evil of Marxism. We are to outdo the commitment of our liberationist friends.

An Ecological Gospel

The Jubilee is the restoration of the land, a restructuring of the human-land relationship. We are to manage the land not to abuse it. To manage, to steward, is to care for, to protect, as well as to develop the productivity of the land. Jesus aim is to bring all of creation out of its bondage and set it free.[55] As the good news of the Jubilee is preached, so the land is allowed to rest. Christians restore and manage the land. But more than that Christians wait for the promised land, the return of the Messiah to rule for "1000 years" (an epoch) and bring right relationships to the land.

Evangelism, this decade, will hinge on Christian leadership of urban and rural environmental issues. As we are working to establish housing for the poor, or to enable a community to raise a sustainable food supply, the reason for our care for the land becomes the centre of our conversation.

The way that the created order can be reinstated to God's original purpose depends upon the proclamation of the Good News.[56] Creation groans until the message of the gospel has penetrated to every nation, every person.[57]

A Celebrating Gospel

In the Jubilee, life becomes a celebration. Even within the simplicity of Jesus' lifestyle, he did not consider things as evil. Jesus knew how to enjoy dining with the rich, yet for the sake of the Kingdom of God, he chose to come to a family who could not afford the dedication offering of the poor.[58] He was accused of being a party-goer - and he was. He loved life and people. This is where he did his evangelism. For as the proclaimer of Jubilee, he was calling people to celebrate.

Our task is to bring the joy of Christ into situations of darkness, the hope of Christ into situations of despair.

A Reconciling Gospel

Immediately after declaring his mandate, Jesus began to talk about ministering to Gentiles. It seems like it was a big mistake! The talk turned from respect for this local son to murder. They tried to murder him! His home town Nazareth was a little Jewish village in the midst of a multicultural context, only four miles from Sapporis, a large Roman centre of about ten thousand citizens, complete with its amphitheatre and public baths. Nazareth had survived by prejudice. His message of God's love for non-Jews went down like a lead balloon, threatening the very foundation of village values.

The Shadow of the Cross on Kiwi-nomics

Which leads us to the centrality of the cross in economic discipleship. For in the cross is the reconciliation of man to God and man to man; in the cross is Jesus' ultimate *detachment* (6) from things of the earth, losing even his own life for the sake of others; in the cross is the principle of *love* (1), of laying down one's life for others, including laying down our possessions; in the cross is the ultimate *work* (4) of God, leading us to consider that works of redemption and reconciliation may be of a higher order than many of our mundane jobs; in the cross we enter into the community of faith, that *economic community* (3) of sharing; in the cross is our *rest* (4), for the anxiety of guilt and sin is laid to rest; in the cross is the principle of giving away, what we have called *redistribution* (7), giving away even our own lives; in the cross his *ownership* (9) of the earth is manifest for he not only redeemed us as and reconciled us as individuals to God but through that the whole creation groans, awaiting his redemption to be complete.[59] All economic principles are integrated in his sacrifice for not just redemption of humanity but the restoration of the earth. It is the most profound economic act of history.

We must speak of this cross to those dealing with economic principles and economic power. These ten principles we have described are central to our message of the gospel. Each calls to repentance. Each calls to obedience to Christ. Each calls to new life, for these ten principles are inherent in the resurrected lives of his people across the nation and hence infiltrate its systems to bring the gospel of liberation from economic sin, and the impending tragedies such sins cause. Each calls to a resurrection to an alternative economics, individually and in terms of new structures.

The Poor in the Kingdom

> *The Spirit of the Lord is upon me, because he has anointed me to preach good news to the poor. He has sent me to proclaim freedom for the prisoners and recovery of sight for the blind, to release the oppressed, to proclaim the year of the Lord's favour* (Luke 4:18, 19).

This was the announcement of Jesus' public ministry in Nazareth. With this choice of scripture Jesus makes clear the job of the herald of the Kingdom and those who are in the Kingdom. Jesus was the incarnate God here to free the poor and proclaim the Kingdom. In this, Jesus lets us know what the Kingdom is about. It is with this announcement we get the first taste of Jesus' economic agenda. The other information that points to Jesus plan are the actions that followed this announcement, namely Jesus ministry. Jesus' ministry following this announcement was exactly like he predicted. Jesus spent most of his time with the poor. He spent much of his time healing the sick and helping the blind see. If we look back on our Old Testament word studies, Jesus, a first century Jew, would know that this scripture from Isaiah was not talking about the spiritually poor, but about those who have been forced into poverty with no way out.

Jesus spent most of his time amongst the poor of his day. It is this and Jesus' teachings that cause James to declare that they, not the rich of this world, will be the heirs of the Kingdom.[60] Jesus taught that it was possible for the rich to enter the Kingdom, but that it was very, very, difficult.[61]

Some of his disciple were poor as well when he chose them. They were called to give up everything for the Kingdom. Jesus also taught his disciples that those who do not care for the poor were not going to be part of his future

Kingdom.[62] Concern for the poor is not an option for the children of the Kingdom it is our central mandate. It is to this standard that we will be judged in the end times.

Dangers of Wealth and Property

> *The poor are blessed,*
> *Poverty is a curse.*
> *The rich are cursed,*
> *Riches are a blessing,*
> *... but very dangerous.*
> *Therefore, we should give them away again.*

Worshipping Possessions

Jesus gave us a choice. He tells us that we *cannot serve God and money*.[63] It is a choice! But *cannot*?! It is an impossible impossibility! Both require one hundred percent commitment. You either love the one and hate the other or you are loyal to one and hate the other. Money never satisfies!

Jesus made the choice. He could have come as rich man or as emperor. But he came to a stable. He could have chosen to be a rich Sadducee but he chose to be a poor wandering scribe.

The rich young ruler made a choice. He could choose wealth or Jesus. He knew it was an either/or choice. He chose his trinkets. He went away sorrowful. *How hard*, Jesus explained to his team, *how hard it is for a rich person to enter the Kingdom of God*.[64]

Covetousness

In the New Testament there is a word used nineteen times.[65] It means striving, desiring material things. It is a greedy compulsion to acquire more and more, the desire to acquire. It is *covetousness which is idolatry...*[66] Why is it idolatry? We desire the thing rather than the creator. Paul commands to *don't even have lunch with another Christian who is ...greedy*,[67] and tells us *the love of money is the root of all evils*.[68] These reflect Jesus, *you cannot serve God and money*.[69]

Spiritual Blindness to Other Needs

Riches are a protection for the rich from the realities of those around him.[70] They may cause him to ignore the needy around him. It was because of this sin that God condemned the rich man in the story of Lazarus and the rich man.[71] The apostle John in old age, tells us, *If anyone has this world's goods and sees his brother in need, yet closes his heart against him, how does God's love abide in him?*[72] Which affirms Jesus, *you cannot love God and money*.[73]

Overwhelmed by Possessions

And *the cares of the age and the delight in riches choke the word, and it proves unfruitful.*[74]

But even within the simplicity of Jesus' lifestyle, he did not consider things as evil, even though as Paul says, *the Kingdom of God does not mean food and drink, but righteousness and joy and peace in the Holy Spirit.*[75]

Jesus, Work and Rest

Christ like the Father , placed a high regard upon work, by labelling himself a worker.[76] He called his disciples to be workers, their work *to be sent out to preach,*[77] to *fish for men.* He prayed for labourers.[78] He also is very familiar with the jobs of the poor and the rich of his time. The use of these parables enabled him to teach in a way that he would be understood, but it also places a high regard upon work. If our work gives glory to God or it serves humanity then it can be seen as a Kingdom job.[79]

Rest is also a key part of life for those who are part of the Kingdom. Leisure can be defined as a time free from the constraints of work and other obligations of living. It is a time to cultivate an enriched state of being.

Jesus was the herald of the Kingdom and he taught us what resting in the Kingdom should look like. The first and foremost leisure time for Jesus was his time of prayer in a lonely place. Jesus, in order to enrich his state of being, turned to his relationship with the Father for help. He knew that this was the priority of the Kingdom when it came to rest. The other form of rest came in the form of fellowship. Jesus loved to spend time both with friends and his disciples. This for him, many times, was his way to rest and he called his disciples to rest with each other.

He had a habit of attending the synagogue on the Sabbath. But in numerous acrimonious debates, he de-legalised the cultural restrictions on rest that the Jewish rabbis had developed in their detailed expansion of the essential command. *The Sabbath is made for man, not man for the Sabbath.*[80]

Ultimately he is our rest. Our hearts are restless, till we find our rest in Him

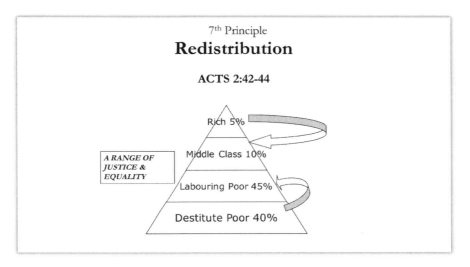

Figure 4: : Jubilee principles demonstrated in the Jerusalem church.

5. Jubilee in the Early Church

In the Old Testament, the economic principles of the Kingdom were seen demonstrated in a nation. In the New Testament, as the church was formative and small, they are demonstrated in communities of believers, communities of the King. We see these worked out within Jesus band of disciples with their common fund, from which they gave to the poor.[1] Then in the first three to four years in their disciples in the Jerusalem church, then in the scattered church plants across Asia Minor towards Rome.

Celebration

The disciples modelled Jesus' principles in the Jerusalem community. Our tenth principle is freedom and celebration. *They partook of food with glad and generous hearts.*[2] The Jerusalem community celebrated life, enjoyed its goodness, but for the sake of their own souls, for the sake of the Kingdom, and for the sake of the needy deliberately forewent their rights.

Cooperative Economics

Acts 2:44 tells us, *all who believed were together and had all things in common.* The fourth principle is *cooperative economics.*

Have you ever wondered why thousands of people started selling their possessions in the early church, so that there was not a needy one among them? The apostles modelled a lifestyle of communal sharing, and of simplicity. This was but an extension of the teaching of Jesus, demonstrated in the common purse of the disciples. It is an extension of the other principle in the Old Testament: *redistribution for equality*, not an utopian equality, but an equality in spirit that results in an active equalizing of resources.

Forsaking

> *And they sold their possessions and goods ...and distributed them to all. as any had need (v. 45).*

When Peter and John went up to the temple and were asked for alms, they had none. So they prayed for healing for the man. This is the nature of a bishop, of a leader of the church, to live simply, and be dependent on God. This involved *forsaking, simplicity, renunciation (6).* The motivation for such drastic action is threefold:

- one cannot serve God and money.
- the needs of proclaiming the Kingdom

- compassion for the poor and needy since, *if anyone has this world's goods and sees his brother in need, yet closes his heart against him, how does God's love abide in him.*[3]

This was *redistribution (7)* to meet the needs of those within the community... The result? a single-mindedness to God, a love for each other and a dynamic witness. We are back to principle one.

Private Ownership Without Possessiveness

Acts 4:32 tells us:

> *the company of those who believed were of one heart and soul, and no-one said that any of the things which they possessed was their own, but they had everything in common.*

Some continued to possess things, but they gave up the attitude of protective *private ownership* (9). It was a voluntary thing. Acts 5 tells us the story of a couple who tried to cheat God. In verse 4, Peter tells them:

> *while the property remained unsold, did it not remain your own? and after it was sold, was it not at your disposal?*

The Equalizing Gospel

In this community we see the *equalizing* (7) effect of the gospel. The poor had their needs met. *There was not a needy one among them.* The rich are brought low. Jesus' brother tells us *Let the believer who is lowly exalt in being raised and the rich in his humiliation.*[4] For the Kingdom uplifts the poor, but the rich refuse to enter it.

But at what level is this equality? Do all of us receive a mansion and two cars? No! it is the level of basic needs. *For we brought nothing into this world and we cannot take anything out of this world, but if we have food and clothing we shall be content.*[5] Basic needs vary according to many factors, so this is not a fixed level - a family of twelve needs more than a single person. It is a voluntary lifestyle. The outward action depends on the inner values.

I used to call it a simple lifestyle but it is a very complex process that is difficult to sustain unless there is a committed community that share this value. For most it is a *sacrificial lifestyle* (6), where we learn to depend on our heavenly Father for our basic needs rather than become anxious.[6] Sacrificial living seems an easier concept to work with.

An Eternal Jubilee?

It is difficult to discern if the early church understood this as simply a year of Jubilee or an eternal Jubilee. We only have a picture of Jerusalem church for three to four years before it was scattered everywhere in Acts 8, so it is difficult to determine what normal church life was beyond those early days of the coming of the Holy Spirit.

On the other hand, since the disciples had been with Jesus for three and a half years living a Jubilee lifestyle, one would likely conclude it was understood as an eternal Jubilee, defining an ongoing lifestyle for the church throughout the ages. That Paul does not refer to the Jubilee is reasonable, as to non-Jews it would have made little sense. (While he preached the Kingdom of God,[7] he only uses that Jewish phraseology sixteen times in his letters, speaking more of its expression in the church or the work of the Holy Spirit).

How then did the early church continue to work out these principles as the gospel expanded?

Work

With a new role to proclaim the Kingdom, and a new community to demonstrate it, do we still need to work? This was the question of the Thessalonians, who were so expectant of Christ's return to establish his Kingdom that they stopped working.

We need to look at both the disciples, called to full-time Christian work and those labouring with their hands, also Christian work. To the latter, Paul instructs, *to aspire to live quietly, to mind your own affairs and to work with your hands, as we charged you; so that you may command the respect of outsiders, and be dependent on nobody.*[8]

Thus we now work for a new set of motivations:

- to extend the Kingdom, by commanding the respect of outsiders.
- to be dependent on nobody and
- to support others,[9] both the needy and those involved in proclaiming the Kingdom.
- The thief must learn to work with his hands (Eph 4:28), so as to give to those in need.

Aside from productive work there are other vocations. Education in the scriptures is always considered good. Knowledge is essential to wisdom. In acquiring knowledge we learn of God. Working at a good education honours God.

Full-time Christian Work

But our primary work is now to be labourers in the Kingdom reaping a harvest.[10]. And some are called to a full-time role in this. A full-time worker is to be supported because of his hard work.[11] *The labourer is worthy of his wages.* However the normal approach of the early church was to depend on laymen and lay elders who supported themselves.

The Old Testament provision of manna, is the basis for Jesus' teaching to the apostles, that they are not to worry about food and drink, for if they *seek first his Kingdom, all these things will be yours as well. Therefore do not worry about tomorrow.*[12] Thus missionary pioneers, both overseas and within New Zealand look to God through prayer for provision. Paul extended this principle numerous times in his writings.

The prophets and the apostles are, it tends to follow this principle of God's supernatural provision, yet with certain communal sanctioning of the processes. The manna is sufficient for the day but not for longer. Though on the sixth day there is provision for the Sabbath.

For the priests (equivalent to today's pastors of local flocks in contrast to the mobile apostles), this is usually well-structured and mandated for the people of God to provide for them regularly through the regular worship – a different process to that of manna. They lived off a portion of the tithe (the majority of the tithes were for the poor, but portions were for the priests). There were various regulations that occurred as the priesthood developed and changed.

Similarly, in the New Testament, the pastor of the local congregation is worthy of *double honour* (i.e. financial remuneration above just honour), especially *those who labour in teaching and preaching.*[13] This is not the young Bible College graduate, who feels entitled to enter a paid job, but the preacher and spouse who have raised their family, provided well for them, and at the same time worthily preached the word. They have seen fruitfulness such that they need to be supported by the church in order to give time to leadership. Denominations develop systems to enable such processes.

William Carey, known as the founder of modern missions, lived by the principle (derived from the Moravians) of *business as mission.* From his business enterprises he supported his apostolic roles and those of his team. Hudson Taylor by contrast, chose to *live by faith*, forming what is now Overseas Missionary Fellowship on the basis of covenant with God that God would provide in answer to prayer alone, coupled with wise communication, but non-solicitation. Both approaches provide an expandable base for new workers to come into the apostolic bands, self-funded, not dependent on past sources of funding.

These are not the same as the fundraising of the American society. Nor are faith missions the same as faith-based organisations of the American society dependent on a whole system of accessing grants from foundations and government, in a government – church symbiosis. This is a worthy process of institutionalised redistribution.

In the Lord's prayer, Jesus teaches us to pray, *give us this day, our daily bread*.[14] In our context, where society is based on monthly or yearly provision, there is sufficient for each month or year.

Thus, those who live by faith are often seen to be struggling. They do not have money put aside. But in reality, they are constantly amazed at the provision of God.

Rest Reinterpreted

Both Paul in the epistles, and the author to the Hebrews reinterpret the principle of rest dramatically. Paul speaks of some holding one day sacred while others in their new found freedom hold all days as being holy.[15] Some would understand him as not speaking of the Sabbath, but of other holy days. Others take this as a liberty to hold all days alike.

Hebrews 4:1-11 speaks of entering our spiritual rest, no longer striving to earn salvation or acceptance, but enjoying the free grace of a salvation bestowed. It is an extension of theme of rest to a perpetual state of rest. As with the rest of the Jubilee principles we are now in continuous Jubilee.

These open the door to a diversity of Christian interpretations. Yet the normative view is to keep Sunday (not a Biblical norm, but a historic cultural choice from Roman times based on celebrating the day of resurrection) as a day of revival through worship (spiritual rest), recreation (physical rest) and restoration (emotional rest), and to seek to sustain national enforcement of this day as beneficial for all – believers or not.

Redistribution

Prov 3:9,10 tells us to give the first fruits of our hands, first and foremost, to God. It is generally considered that the tithe is a workable amount to give, though the New Testament nowhere commands this. As my father used to say,

> *Give 10%, save 10%, then live within your means.*

The first priority with the tithe is giving to the poor. In the New Testament the portion for the poor was given to the apostles, who distributed through the deacons to the poor.

A portion of the tithe was to be used for the priest (the equivalent in many churches today being the minister or pastor). But not the whole tithe – many of our churches consume most of the giving on pastoral salaries and buildings rather than delivery of services to the needy. Only a tithe of the tithe was given to sustain the temple and priests. Yet, while we no longer have a temple, we also have a collective responsibility for sustaining our worship places and pastoral leaders.

It cannot be affirmed that the Old Testament law of tithes is binding on the Christian Church in the New Testament, nevertheless the principle of this law remains, and is incorporated in the gospel.[16] If the motive to liberality is greater now than in Old Testament times, then Christians ought to go beyond the Jewish people in consecrating both themselves and their substance to God.

There is no teaching on tithing in the New Testament. But there is teaching on sacrificial giving. A good starting point for giving is to follow the Old Testament principle of tithing for the poor, plus a tithe of a tithe for the full time Christian workers, such as pastors. We can move money to the poor as we have workers among the poor, so the support of missionaries is a critical part of our redistribution.

The location of where that giving goes is complex, and very culturally defined. Many pastors believe the tithe should be given to the church. In the book of Acts, it was given to the Apostles for redistribution. Today apostles lead large movements, so there is a basis for giving and redistributing through the denominational structures. The apostle Paul, appreciated very much the Philippian gifts to his mission work.[17]

From all of the above it canbe seen that there is no one way that finaincial structures should be developed in churches and denominations and misisons, but there are clusters of principles.

There are also aberrations I face globally among the poor. Poor pastors struggle to survive, so put more and more pressure on their poor people to give. This is supported by the Prosperity Gospel, which says if they give to this pastor's need, God will bless. There is a question as to whether one must first provide for one's family. In the Pacific Island community, as in poor communities globally, the pressures to give to the church can be very intense where in the words of one of my friends, people beg, borrow or steal at times to contribute to the church!! This ought not to be! The widow's mite is to be voluntarily given, not coerced!

Jubilee and International Redistribution

The principles of Jubilee as evidenced in Jesus' apostolic community, then in the Acts community, are further extended globally in Paul's teaching on global redistribution between the churches in II Cor 8, 9. What does this mean for us? We are to share from our resources so that others are uplifted, so all come to some level of equality and justice. God didn't intend exact equality but he did intend justice and levels that feel equal and free and creative.

We can marry this principle seven of *redistribution* with the principle of social justice into a principle of *distributive justice at national levels*. There will never be a clear Christian consensus as to the extent Government should be involved in such distributive justice as it is a balancing act between the Biblical imperative, affirmed multiple times in the Psalms, for rulers to make sure the poor are provided for, and the Biblical theme of limits on the authority of government which the prophet Samuel enumerated. Penk[18] and Thomas[19] seek to balance these principles in their evaluations of the New Zealand taxation regime. Throughout the last century, most theologians have argued for the importance of governmental care for the poor. Right-wing American theologians tend to err towards limiting government involvement.

Simple Lifestyle vs Addictive Consumption

> *But godliness with contentment is great gain. For we brought nothing into the world, and we can take nothing out of it. But if we have food and clothing, we will be content with that.*[20]

Jesus tells us to step out of the world, the desire for other things, the delight in riches. Addiction to consumption requires drastic surgery if we are to be holy. Generally we use the phrase a *Lifestyle of Simplicity* to speak of the Kingdom opposite to the greed that controls our society. This principle has been developed for Kiwis going to live in the slums in my earlier writings, *The Lifestyle and Values of Servants*, and follows,[21] See also Murray Sheard's work, *Living Simply,* for an expansion of these ideas.[22]

Non-Destitute Poverty

> *The Master not only chose poverty in birth, in life and death, he also calls his servants to such a lifestyle. We recognize our basic needs for food and clothing (I Timothy 6:6-8, Matthew 6:25-33), which may include tools of our trade, children's toys.*

> *We recognize the just need, inferred from the Scriptures for each family to own its own home, although some, like the Master, may choose a mobile, apostolic*

life with nowhere to lay one's head *(Luke 9:58)*. In putting our treasure in heaven, we covet the unsearchable riches of Christ.

We desire to possess nothing that cannot be shared with those around us. Regarding what we have, we hold it not as our own but rather as lent to us for a season. We will seek to exclude from both our personal and communal lives the cares of the world, the delight in riches and the desire for other things *(Matthew 4:19)*.

We will avoid the abundance of communal properties or wealth. Buildings, administration and ministry shall be developed in the simplest manner consistent with good health and with efficient, well-pleasing work.

3. Inner Simplicity

Renouncing possessions is an outworking of an inner simplifying of our lives which lead to the openness, gentleness, spontaneity, and serenity that marked the Master.

In renouncing possessions, we seek to simplify our external lives in order to simplify more clearly our inner lives and focus on knowing our Lord.

Along with outward poverty, we desire an inner humility; along with servant works, we seek the spirit of a true servant.

In caring little for this world where we are strangers and pilgrims, we set our hearts on that spiritual home where our treasure is being saved up, and on that glory which we shall share with our Lord, provided we suffer with him.

We encourage middle-class Christians to such simplicity of lifestyle. For some it means earning less, and using their time for the kingdom.

For others it means to earn much, consume little, hoard nothing, give generously and celebrate living. Such lifestyles are infinitely varied. We refuse to judge others in such areas.

The Choice

What is the action you need to take regarding finances? Is it to make the basic decision to put first his Kingdom? Is it to get out of the terrible grasp of riches or debt? Is it forsaking all, in order that you might proclaim the gospel? Is it to work harder in order to help those in need? Is it to share the possessions you have?

God is very creative. There are many alternatives. Which is the alternative he is speaking to you?

The following chart summarises the *Ten Principles of Economic Discipleship*. Each principle stems from the nature of God in Genesis 1, is seen in the Jubilee in Leviticus 23, is part of Jesus' teaching and lifestyle, is reproduced in the Acts community, and is taught by Paul in the epistles. Each situation is different, but the principles remain consistent across the time frame of redemption history. In Part 2, we will integrate some of these themes, and begin to engage them in a conversation with the present Kiwi context. In Part 3, we will seek to define the national *conversation space* to engage with some current issues in the light of these principles

Ten Principles of Economic Discipleship				
Principle	**Genesis**	**Pentateuch Jubilee**	**Gospels**	**Early Church**
1. Love & Tthe Worth of each Individual	Created in God's image	Laws that protect the poor, the migrant, the widow	Care for the lame, blind, needy, widows	Care for widows, orphans
2. Creativity	God the creator		Truth will set you free	Spirit sets free
3. Productivity	Good outcomes	6years and 49 years of productivity	Parables of multiplying seed as a Kingdom principle	Work with your hands[1]
4.Cooperation	Let *us* make	Laws including the marginalised	Common purse, Not a needy one among them	Provide for others[2]
5. Work & Rest	He makes He structures God rests, Sabbath rest	Sabbath, Jubilee rest	Jubilee come[3] Labour in the gospel	Jubilee. Work with hands,[4] provide for family and needy. Eternal rest
6. Detachment & Simplicity			Consider lilies and birds.[5] Sell possessions.[6] Forsake all[7]	I become all things to all men.[8] Be content.[9]
7.Redistribut'n for Equality	Abraham tithes	Jubilee –return of land	Give to him who asks	Not a needy one. Global redist'n[10] Role of a deacon
8.Management, Savings & Debt	Manage the earth.	Land needs rest, Jubilee cancels debts	Parables of stewardship. Forgive us our debts	Owe no person, Simplicity
9. Freedom & Celebration	It was good	Blow trumpet	Declare liberty! The truth shall set you free[11]	Freedom of Spirit, liberty of private ownership
10. Ownership & Property Rights	Each family to own their own home	Each family to be given back land.	Forsake all, yet own home[12]	Provide for family[13]

Figure 4: Completed chart of ten principles of economic discipleship

Figure 5: How do we interpret Kingdom economic themes into the 1450 mostly multicultural churches, and multiple economic strata of Auckland, economic driver of Pacific Island commerce.

Part 2: Integrating the Themes

In part 2, we integrate some of these Biblical principles and do some initial conversation with three issues in the New Zealand context: *management* (8) and technology principles; *co-operation* (4) and co-operative economic structures as alternatives to Capitalism; land rights and *land ownership* (9) in our Maori-Pakeha dance.

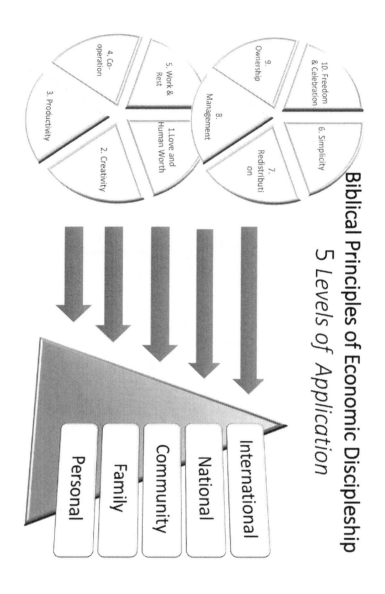

Figure 6: Five Levels of Application: The first half of this book has applied Biblical principles to personal, family and community level economics. The second half applies it to national and international economic issues.

6. Biblical Financial Management Principles

Managing Resources and Technology

In Godzone country, where the grass grows, sheep eat the grass and we grow rich, questions abound for most of us. How do I manage the money God has given me? How do I increase it? How do I spend it? What about debts? savings? insurance? partnerships?

Real estate and our industries are morphing into something far more complex than in the past. And there are many financial structures that the middle class access, that are not discussed in the scriptures – retirement, share markets, bonds, insurance, risk management, mortgages… It is important to know the Biblical principles, but then we need to be very careful to interpret them into the new environment of the technological nation in which we live.

Meanwhile other leaders in business are under constant need of supportive governmental frameworks that enable them to be competitive in the global market. For if they misstep they perish as the balance their *creativity* in development of new products with the needs of *production* at a level that continues to bring in a reasonable profit for those who have invested in their company and can sustain the consistent needs of their workforce in a godly manner. If such economic leaders fail to *manage* and keep pace with the global realities, we all lose. The evolution of a model of a mixed economy largely following capitalist principles is essential in the midst of these diverse pressures.

Our Principle 8, *financial management* is *the wise allocation of the monetary resources that God has dispensed to us for the maximum extension of the Kingdom of God.* This includes avoiding debt, not charging usurious interest rates, not entering partnerships with unbelievers, and a host of financial management skills. We will expand the underlying Biblical themes, and comment on some ways these impinge the structuring of a debt-based economy. Financial management programs abound for families, so we will not venture into these. MBA's at business level are a highly refined art that builds from the Biblical principles that underlie our Western culture, though rarely referencing them.

Biblical Principles of Financial Management for Families

From Genesis, we can build some foundations for a theology of management. First, God is the *Giver* of all things because he is the *Creator* of all things,[1] and therefore He is the *Owner* of all things.[2] Despite our sin, He has freely given us salvation through his own Son and through Him also he has provided us with all our needs.[3]

He has delegated to humanity the rights and responsibilities of having dominion over the earth and all living creatures. People are *managers* on behalf of God, accountable to God and required to rule as God would have him rule. They own nothing but have everything on trust. They are God's stewards on earth.

From the Wisdom literature we also learn the need for wisdom in handling money matters – accountants like the phrase prudence. Solomon, the wisest and richest King in Israel likely collated the book of Proverbs so that men and women might know wisdom. Many of these proverbs relate to management. Wisdom is the ability to understand the situation, anticipate consequences and therefore, make sound decisions. It is a rare combination of discretion, maturity, keenness of intellect, broad experience, extensive learning, profound thought and compassionate understanding. But true wisdom begins with the fear of the Lord. And the right kind of fear is that which springs out of a true love for the Lord. It is standing in awe of him.

The allocation of resources requires planning in order to control their use and misuse as well as to give attention to the different needs according to priorities. All plans should be committed to the Lord.[4] For this reason we're told to *develop your business first, before building your home.*[5]

These proverbs continue through the New Testament. Jesus also used parables. What then are some qualities of a steward (or manager) as mentioned in Jesus and the Epistles? They are faithful and wise, honest, trustworthy[6] and employ God's given blessings for others' welfare and good and not only for their own.[7]

In practice, first take out your tithe.

> *While reading some patristic documents recently I was startled to discover that the Church Fathers are univocal in their insistence that the bulk of the revenue collected by a local church belonged by right to the poor. There was no expectation among them that a large percentage of what was collected by a local congregation would be used for its own maintenance and ministry. In fact, to do so would have been viewed by them as a misappropriation of funds.*[8]

The amount left needs to be allocated according to priorities as an effective steward. It is here that many problems arise. Often, because we have given to God first, we think God will bless us and then we spend our money on anything we feel we need and desire. An effective steward is one who plans on how best they can benefit from what they have now.

We do not work for their own luxury and selfish enjoyment. We need enough money to (1) care for family and relatives.[9] (2) To pay taxes and other payments imposed by the government.[10]

In our training in the third world we then work with people to keep a daily record of spending. One accountant friend who hosted me in Auckland, when asked what was the most important step in managing finances, replied, *keeping a daily record of expenses*. Based on that they prepare *a weekly or monthly budget*. In time this leads to a recording of monthly *income and expenses* and the development of a *balance sheet*. There are Christian budgeting services in New Zealand that can assist with these issues.

Debts & Loans

The basic principle is to *owe no one anything*,[11] since *the borrower is servant of the lender*.[12] So if you can pay your debts do so today.[13] There is no *pautang-utang* (a Filipino debt of gratitude, it doesn't need repayment at least for now, but it remains in the back of our minds) in the Kingdom of God. We are to work to support ourselves, to live within our means, and we are to look after our poor.

Charitable Loans

In lending to a poor believer we are to lend without interest,[14] since *they who are kind to the poor, lend to the Lord*.[15] Indeed, Jesus takes the principle of giving generously even further. We should *lend, expecting nothing in return*,[16] being unconcerned with the fact that it cannot be repaid. Good will come to those who lend freely, conducting their affairs with justice.[17] There is no 5:6 in the Kingdom of God (Indian money lenders in the Manila slums lend five pesos today and you must repay six pesos tomorrow). If a poor person is so poor that the only collateral they have is their coat, return it to them that day.[18]

Since the poor get poorer and eventually become slaves, the Lord commanded periodic cancelling of debts and release of those who had been enslaved.[19]

Don't make loans to strangers,[20] and don't countersign a note unless you have extra cash.[21]

Commercial Loans

Notice that all the above instructions are in the context of lending to help people get out of *personal poverty*. It appears that at the time of the Exodus and on into the Monarchy borrowing capital for business was not highly practiced.

In modern society, commercial loans are considered as a way of giving money to a person to manage for a fixed length of time. This person through business of investment is to make money - enough for himself and enough to repay the back capital plus interest. It is a contract between borrower and lender that benefits both.

Do not borrow on depreciating asset (i.e. on things that will decrease in value) since the loan will not increase your money and you will be unable to pay it back (e.g. do not borrow money to buy a motorcycle for personal use since it decreases in value yearly). On the other hand, if you borrow to buy land or a motorcycle to extend your business contacts you will make money, since land over time usually increases in value and business contacts bring more income). If this advice to weigh risks carefully is followed Rom 13:8 will be fulfilled to *owe no one anything.*

> *O Peter don't you call me, cause I can't go,*
> *I owe my soul to the company store.*

Usury and Sub-Prime Lending

The historic term, *usury*, in the scriptures means giving loans to the poor. It has come to mean loans at excessive interest rates, that push people further and further into debt. This is forbidden in the scriptures.

It is forbidden to exact usury from your poor brother.[22] We are to give to the poor and not expect interest on the payback. St Jerome (340-420) argued that the term brother had been universalised by the Prophets and New Testament. Thus there is no basis for taking usury from anyone. St Ambrose (340-397), in contrast, proposed a clear discrimination against the enemy, the alien, the outsider. But as Max Weber describes, the evolution of Europe from tribal to universal man, indicates the application of the principle for all becomes reasonable.[23]

The church historically has declared it to be reprehensible to make money by lending at interest. The early church fathers, and canonical laws of the Middle Ages absolutely forbade the practice. There is a most enjoyable or perhaps horrific story of the wanderings of a Catholic priest who had spoken in his churches against usury and been dismissed by his bishop from preaching. He wandered back and forth from Ireland to France to the Pope and the Americas in order to have the church disprove what he had written which then became a standard text. *Usury is destructive of that equality ordained by common sense and reason in the dealings of man with man...against the law of nature.*[24]

When I have spoken against the evils of Capitalism in various contexts, some good friends have taken me to task. "Capitalism is Christian!" they tell me. But I dig out old books, and the histories of Capitalism from the prolific English author of fifty books on economics, including a classic on Imperialism, John A Hobson (1927), developing his English economic history off the seven hundred page history by German sociologist and economist, Sombart (1902), [25] indicates that nearly all of the processes of amassing capital during the foundational shifts from feudalism to Capitalism were exploitative, beginning with the papal treasury in Rome, and the knightly orders with their pillaging and plundering, the royal treasuries of France and England and the higher grades of feudal nobility who gained their treasures by rents. The exception is those families (the burghers) that were originally in possession of ground in which towns were built, and hence over time could control rents and mill and markets - to some extent through relatively just means.

Surplus capital is the foundation. From these feudal contexts, the discovery of precious metals through global conquest or piracy, enabled the formation of the business class. But to fund such wars, and sustain the role of nobility, moneylenders were essential. In England, these were first Jewish (not subject to the church's ban on usury), then Italian, and by the sixteenth Century, English families. But it was colonialism that fuelled Capitalism:

> *The exploitation of other portions of the world through military plunder, unequal trade, and forced labour has been the one great indispensable condition of the growth of European capitalism ... the previous destruction of Arab civilization, the plundering of Africa, the impoverishment and desolation of Southern Asia and its island world, the fruitful East Indies, and the thriving states of the Incas and Aztecs.*[26]

This is a statement of a sage economic historian, over one hundred years ago, closer to those dynamics than we are. Thus, to be emotional when one speaks of usury, exploitation, colonialism and Capitalism is not irrational. Some roots of Capitalism may be Christian according to Tawney and Weber, but history tells of a dark side from its inception, that must be resisted and controlled.

In addition to capital, the global exploitation resulted in the slave trade providing the second leg of Capitalism, cheap labour, as the migration from the rural peasants to the cities was not sufficient in itself, to fuel the full emergence of the British Capitalist enterprise. This condition continues to this day, with the in-migration of labour from poorer nations being essential to any nation's expansion of industry.

Calvin took a different approach to usury to that of historic Christianity. He taught that lending money with interest was not wrong in principle, but that extortion that goes along with it was wrong. He prohibited excessive interest or lending that did injury to a neighbour. Thus, he bestowed a religious endorsement on the principle of credit.

The Catholic church claims its doctrine has not changed...

> *The change in the attitude in Calvin and of the Church since the 1700's is due entirely to a change in understanding of the nature of money by the present*

system, not any change to a prohibition on usury. [The Catholic]Church itself now puts its funds out at interest, and requires administrators to do the same.[27]

Max Weber, in *The Protestant Work Ethic and the Spirit of Capitalism* indicates a cluster of teachings and values that resulted from Calvin's teaching. Along with this change related to usury at a structural level, Calvin taught about a God-ordained destiny for some to fulfil their vocations in business, their success demonstrating their salvation, and affirmed qualities of thrift, diligence, sobriety, frugality. Religion thus became harnessed to economic development.

But over the last decades, this now common understanding that interest is acceptable, but excessive interest is not, has faced new challenges with the creation and expansion of new forms of credit.

The prime sector in the US banking system is where loans are made to those with clear credit histories determined by inflexible computer programs in three large credit rating agencies. In contrast, the US sub-prime sector is a significant sector of the population who have bad credit, immigrants who cannot get credit, or those who have never accessed the credit system. It has gained wide notoriety as a result of the part it played in precipitating a crisis in the global credit market. Mortgage loans made in the United States with insufficient regard to borrowers' ability to pay were sold on to other investors in a secondary market— and when the underlying loans were found to be of much less value than expected, many financial institutions found themselves under severe pressure. This caused the 2008 downturn.

There is a flip side to the system. We have had the experience of entering the United States and despite a good income and years of good credit in New Zealand being denied credit because we are not in the credit system of the three credit rating companies that control US bank decisions. Excluded from bank credit, and with initial high costs through the move till the first pay checks start coming, how then do you obtain loans for your initial car to get travelling (a necessity in LA) or a house. It is a situation of oppression (control by three companies based on execution of computer programs with no face) and exclusion from the US economy. We could not enter the *prime* banking system.

Sub-prime lending is lending directed to those who do not meet these computerised conventional criteria of credit-worthiness. The traditional sub-prime market, referred to in the UK as 'home credit', is the offering of small unsecured loans at high interest rates to consumers with low incomes, with repayments often collected door-to-door on a weekly basis. Sub-prime secured lending provides mortgage and home equity loans secured on property to those who have difficulty in obtaining credit elsewhere.

In New Zealand, there has also been a multiplicity of largely unregulated loan shark shops being set up in corners in poorer suburbs. Unsecured money of a few hundred to a few thousand dollars is easy to get before payday – at usurious interest rates. This occurs in all countries in poor areas. A nation needs constant vigilance to protect the poor and wisdom to provide support for the poor.

Access to and use of consumer credit has also expanded enormously over recent decades through the expansion of the credit card industry, again controlled by global companies, charging interest rates which by historic global standards are *usurious*. This wider use of credit accentuates the exclusion from society experienced by those who cannot access mainstream credit facilities. If you cannot pay off your credit card in a given month, you then start paying interest. At that point you should cut it up.

High fees by the lenders in most cases fall within the historic category of charging usurious interest (often hidden in excessive fees). Many experienced this in New Zealand when the banks charged exorbitant break fees (fees to re-mortgage at cheaper rates) once the interest rates dropped – the small print on these was so small that you needed bifocals to read it. In a report in April 2006, the General Board of Pension and Health Benefits of the United Methodist Church in the UK advanced a definition of predatory lending:

> *Predatory lending is a form of subprime lending characterized by unscrupulous or unethical lending practices. These practices can include the application of excessively high fees and interest rates, the use of balloon payments, flipping (successive refinancing of the original loan at increasingly higher rates), packing (linking the issuance of the loan to the purchase of some form of insurance) and steering (directing otherwise credit-worthy borrowers into high-priced subprime loans). Predatory lending tends to target certain segments of society, most often the elderly, the poor and minorities. The United Methodist Church has directed all general agencies to invest in banks that have 'policies and practices that preclude predatory or harmful lending practices.* [28]

Partnerships

We are not to be mismated to unbelievers in marriage.[29] Most Christian businessmen understand that this applies to business also. In a partnership, all partners take responsibility for management decisions. If your partner is not a Christian, you cannot be sure of their honesty, and certainly they will not be seeking as their primary objective to extend the Kingdom of God, through their business dealings. This does not mean we do not work under or employ non-Christians or relate to them. The issue here is one of responsibility for decisions.

Similarly, full time pastors not to get entangled in civilian pursuits,[30] since we are involved in the work of ministry. Entanglement in business contracts can be deadly for those called to ministry, but also for those within business circles.

Management of Savings

It is the later wisdom literature at the time of an urban society that expands on the nature of work and with it the pattern of building savings. Life is lived in cycles. There is a time to save and a time to spend.[31] We all save, even if we only save our salary for a few days. We are to follow the example of the ant;[32] during a time of abundance, we should put aside money for the lean years. *The wise person saves for the future, but the foolish spends whatever he gets.*.[33]

The principle behind savings is consistency. You have to stick at it. After a while it becomes second nature. Some people teach give 10% to the Lord's work, save 10% and budget the rest for the present needs.

Life Stages

As incomes increase, consumption tends to increase proportionally. We have to keep a shrewd eye on how to live simply, and maximize savings, and giving at every stage of life.

The first difficulty is debt funding of tertiary education. A degree is now regarded as essential for survival in the knowledge society, and New Zealand has rapidly been extending its tertiary education options. A generation ago, while studying Engineering at Canterbury University, and working every vacation day in sheep shearing, fruit picking, delivering sacks of coal, internships in electronics companies, plus a small bursary, I could complete my degree without debt. Despite government support keeping fees for New Zealanders at lower levels than most other countries, and if a student is working 10 hours per week at minimum wage, this is now nearly impossible. At minimum, youth end up with $5000 per year of debt. It is critical to immediately pay down that debt, once one is earning.

With the increased income from a degree, the next hurdle is the cost of a wedding, traditionally funded by parents, but often this is not fully an option. If you know you will get married, you should be saving for it. In New Zealand, once you can buy a house to live in, your money will generally continue to increase, so the collective wisdom of the generations has been to save for this first. Set aside also a certain percentage for emergencies such as sickness, unexpected guests, or deaths.

Paying off your first mortgage month by month is a great expense. Thus you are engaged in the systems of finance of the country. And there is not a lot of room to wriggle. With good management, and God's blessing, the systems should enable you to survive well within the cultural *milieu*. Once paying off a mortgage instead of paying rent, you are likely saving.

Most families can then increase income and wealth through time. It is preferable to own your own business, if you can succeed than to be an employee. Despite the abuses of global capitalism, in the mixed New Zealand economy, these are all good things –provided we have done some research into ethical investing in companies that do not undermine our belief system.

In our society, retirement savings are essential. Within the guidelines of the above principles there are many options for savings of funds in banks, stocks, bonds, real estate, currency within the modern economy.

If older, likely your employer has asked you to monthly pay into some insurance scheme and some retirement scheme. You are having to manage stocks and bonds, with little knowledge of who is benefiting from your money. A wise person looks ahead and plans for kids' university and retirement in culturally acceptable ways, for they see hard times and plan for them.[34] But greed is despised:[35] we don't need to save a great nest egg for some unknown future calamity.

There is a great deal of teaching available as to how one can engage in these markets. There are funds which meet criteria for ethical investment, though one has to be careful as even the most immoral companies seem to find a way to proclaim they are involved in ethical investing. I was looking at one ethical investment portfolio on the stock market the other day, and noticed Pepsi was listed. It certainly provides drinks in the slums where the water is no good. On the other hand, those drinks can dissolve a nail, so they say - I have not done the experiment -so is marketing a faulty product to the world's poor globally make it an ethical company? It would be outside the brief of this paper to engage in an analysis of these, applying the principles above.

The godly man thus provides for his retirement, for his widow and leaves an inheritance for his children.[36] Churches need to provide systems of support in financial decisions like these, and in budgeting processes. The modern state needs to provide stable infrastructure to sustain employment, accessible house prices that enable home ownership for all, and education that does not end up with a generation in deep debt.

7. The Cooperative Principle

Sometimes by looking at other contexts we can better see ourselves. This chapter deviates to the Christian leadership of the cooperative principle in transforming urban poor global realities. The contrast may spark off thoughts as to appropriate developments in New Zealand.

Examining these principles from experinces in the global slums leads one to consider parallel issues required for an OECD nation. Ultimately, development economists have come up with complex lists of elements that lead to both rising incomes and harmonious societies with levels of income equality.[1] This chapter will examine the nature of cooperatives as the basis of capital formation. This leads to an integration of the poor into the macro-economic systems.

Cooperation as the Basis of Capital Formation

What is remarkable in reviewing economic theologies over the last two hundred years, is the recurrence of the theme of *cooperative economics* vs. Capitalism vs. Marxism. It should not be remarkable, as the church at its outset was a cooperative economic community. And that was based on Jesus' travelling band with their common purse. Europe was saved in the middle ages by communities of faith following those same practices.[2]

> God is an *usness*, a cooperative community

It begins in the *usness* of God. He is a cooperative community. It reflects the Acts 2 community and their cooperative economic processes. It has been the basis of many experiments in community in New Zealand. In the uplift of the global urban poor, for the last thirty years it has kept surfacing as a critical principle for building capital among poor people.

This principle is partially developed within Capitalism in the structure of companies: boards, partnerships, work teams; and in Communism in cooperative efforts controlled by the Party; but as Christians we focus on *dispersion of power to alternative grassroots economic communities*. Christian communities, churches where wealth is shared, Kingdom banks, cooperatives and microfinance processes among the poor globally.

Cooperatives as Basis for Kiwi Wealth

In New Zealand, despite their lack of publicity, as there is no daily "market" news about them, cooperatives have been one of the keys to prosperity. In 2007, the combined turnover of cooperatives and mutuals in New Zealand was over $27bn, representing 21% of the country's gross domestic product. They range from a cooperative of mobile phone retailers which has just over 20 members, through the dairy co-op which is by far the country's largest commercial business with 11,000 farmer members, to a financial services cooperative with a little under 140,000 members – to say that cooperative and mutual business is important here is an understatement. Member-owned businesses whose shares are not traded on the stock exchange, most cooperatives keep a low profile.

There are complex issues in developing cooperatives just as in any business. Trust is a crucial issue in the early formation, and is easier come by in a tight-knit ethnic community. Fonterra as a multinational corporation faces limitations on capital as the farmers are limited in their resources. Other New Zealanders would like to share the wealth generated but are excluded...

A cooperative is[3] *an organisation owned by and democratically operated for the benefit of those using its services.* The activities can be virtually any legal business operation provided for in the rules of the cooperative, and may be for the supply of goods or services to members and/or for the supply of goods or services to others. In some ways, cooperatives operate much like any other business, but they do have a number of unique characteristics.

- Member ownership: The member-owners share equally in the control of their cooperative, meeting at regular intervals to review detailed reports and elect directors from among themselves.
- Open membership – anyone who wants to become a member can do so, though some are targeted to specific populations.
- Democratic control – members control the cooperative by electing its board of directors
- Ownership rebates – margins or earnings are returned to members in proportion to the amount of business done with the cooperative
- Continuing cooperative education – a duty to educate members and the public in general about our cooperative form of business as a unique and valuable part of the private enterprise system
- Cooperation among cooperatives – working together is one of the strengths of cooperatives
- Concern for community – while focusing on members' needs, co-ops work for the sustainable development of their communities through policies approved by their members

The Original Rochdale Principles

During the 1840's in the UK, at a place called Rochdale in Lancashire (near Manchester), pioneers were establishing a trading business in basic commodities of flour, sugar, wheat etc. on the basis of giving fair and accurate measure for the purchase. Such fairness in trading had been lacking with unscrupulous traders giving short measure and poor quality of goods, like having chalk in the flour. From the development of the Rochdale business came a set of business principles which were adopted and extended into various forms of business.

The operation of cooperatives was quick to catch on in many countries and a considerable period of growth ensued. The concept was widely adopted and emerged in many countries of the world. The first general cooperative was formed in New South Wales, Australia in 1859 and since then cooperatives developed throughout Australia.

One of the most successful cooperative endeavours, perhaps the most famous, is the Mondragon Group in Spain's Basque country. This began in 1956 in the town of Mondragon and enormous businesses have been developed through the widespread adoption of the cooperative business model. This is a worker cooperative, which is owned collectively by those who work for the cooperative. To this day, it is a model example of how cooperative business can operate for the success of the people who own it.

There are strong cooperatives in most countries in Europe. With the changes taking place in the Chinese economy, there are moves for state-owned businesses to move to ownership by the people who participate and thereby become fully-fledged cooperatives. A little known fact is that in the USA, bastion of what is known as the free market, cooperatives provide half a million jobs with the six largest cooperative sectors counting 21,367 co-ops that serve nearly 130 million members, or 43 per cent of all Americans.

Diffusion of Power

A reading of the above may identify an underlying agenda from the scriptures, the imperative for *diffusion of decision-making power, and the dignity of the individual as a basis for affirming the equality of each person*. The first theme is highlighted in the debate between the prophet Samuel with the people who wanted a King. He talks about the evils of centralisation of power and its invariable oppression and exploitation of the people. Societies are strong to the extent that the exercise of power is consistently pushed towards the grassroots. The multiplication of small organisations, be they religious, economic or political strengthen the

> **Diffusion of Power**
>
> Multiplication of small religious, economic, social and political entities diffuses power and enables leadership formation.

decision-making of society. This principle is based on creation, that each person is created of equal and infinite worth. The prince is not better than the pauper. The executive is not better than the labourer.

How the Poor Escape Poverty

When one works among the poor, the question to ask is not, "What can we do for the poor?" but "How do the poor themselves escape poverty and how can we assist in this?"

There are seven main answers that may surprise you: conversion and discipleship in communities (church growth); migration; education, particularly vocational education; cooperative capital formation, land rights and health care. These could be restated as formation of spiritual capital; relocation to contexts of capital; skills capital; economic capital formation; collective political capital, and capitalizing land. Health care, perhaps restated as health capital undergirds ability to do these. Multiplication of small religious, economic, social and political entities diffuses power and enables leadership formation.

Religious life is crucial. Multiplication of churches – Christian communities is a basis of creation of power centres that in many countries are the only contexts that can oppose oppression. Churches are central in the creation of new motivated lifestyles, social communities and networks and the formation of economic capital through forming cooperatives. They are significant in the formation of leadership that can enter into the social and political arenas. The teaching of the church on God as a cooperative being; its training in the character of working in unity; its teaching of the ten economic principles of this study; its teaching on seeking justice and opposing injustice lays a basis for these structural developments. The gospel results in capital formation, slowly at first. There is a phrase in missiology: redemption and lift.[4] Over one to two generations those poor who are converted, discipled and formed into churches rise up economically because of motivation, perfectionism, hard work, and education.

Wealth Formation and Uplift of a Poor People

We teach the following in the *MA in Transformational Urban Leadership*[5] and some of our grassroots urban poor trainers teach these in the slums around the world.

Among the poor there is money. But there is not access to capital for starting of small businesses that will generate money. The solution to this is the development of cooperative savings schemes. When a group of people put their small amounts week by week into a common fund it grows to a significant amount of capital which can then be given to one of the members of the group to start a small business. This person then can repay that loan week by week, while the continued process of group savings continues till the next person can be given a capital loan, and so on till the whole group have had access to the capital. At that point, they are all earning more, so the amount of loans moves up a step to the next level of capitalisation.

Along with education or migration, this is one of the significant ways that poor people escape poverty. The process can be accelerated by injection of funds from outside at appropriate levels. Over the last thirty years, a significant set of procedures have been developed in many places round the world to facilitate such processes called *microfinance*.

We teach a certain progression:

Conversion: As discussed under the section on productivity earlier, conversion (not to religion but experiencing forgiveness of sins, and turning from them to seek goodness), revival (the experience of a living God) and discipleship (following disciplines of holiness) are all critical to the formation of the essential character of successful workers and entrepreneurs. Integrity, thrift, hard work, sense of vocation, sense of identity, motivation to excellence are all the fruit of conversion, and seeking to follow Christ and the research on entrepreneurs indicate these are essential characteristics of successful entrepreneurs.

Community of Faith: Loving others, serving others, having the heart of a servant, working cooperatively, in unity, being part of and learning to build teams are crucial leadership skills learned in the life of a healthy church. Building social capital occurs as does the relationships for building small economic groups.

Cooperative Savings: There are two types of savings groups or Self Help Groups (SHG's, our simplest and hence best introduction to this is a little booklet by the International Labour Organization[6] that have become recognised internationally as assisting the poor out of poverty through capital formation, ASCA's and ROSCA's, where clusters of twenty or more people pay into a common savings fund weekly or monthly.

Cooperative Capital: Once a group has demonstrated faithfulness in savings, managing the money, and have built some capital, then they are in a position to loan to one of their members. That member can invest that into making more money so are able to repay at a higher rate than just the monthly savings. Thus, producing the capital for the next person takes a shorter space of time. Within time, every person in the group has been given capital and capitalised the next phase of their business.

Developing Business Skills: At this point in the progression, success is often dependent on mentoring and skills training. Vocational training is a major asset.

Micro-Finance: Based on a track record of savings, loans and repayment of capital, such groups are now able to demonstrate to banks or Micro-Finance groups that they are a good credit risk and obtain access to larger capital amounts. This is both good - and problematic, as it is based on a debt model not a savings model. Banks exist to put people into debt. They make money off debt and interest. But if the money is well used to make money, and the risks have been well evaluated, then this access to capital can set people free. I have seen both success and failure. This contrasts with the savings groups where almost all are positive stories.

Migration: At any point in this progression if a person can move from a resource-poor geography to an asset rich location, they are more likely to end up with productive work and income.[7] The migration process is fraught with danger and potential for failure. Long-term it usually creates opportunity and success, though with much struggle and emotional dislocation.

Varieties of Cooperative Groups

> ### How Do the Poor Escape Poverty?
>
> **Spiritual Capital:** Conversion and discipleship, communities of faith
>
> **Financial Capital:** cooperative capital formation.
>
> **Skills Capital:** vocational education.
>
> **Location Capital:** migration to places with resources.
>
> **Housing Capital:** obtaining land tenure and hence developing collateral for capital loans.
>
> **Health Capital:** All this is built on good health care.

Self-Help Groups[8]

There are many types of cooperative savings groups. Some band together to cover funeral costs through weekly savings, or for other large expenses like weddings or births or illnesses

Others are vehicles for capital accumulation for business formation. In New Zealand the Vietnamese and Cambodians group into ten families and put savings into a co-operative fund called a *thong*. They all give money to one family to buy a bakery. Then to the next, till all have bakeries!! Ask about it next time you want a cream bun!

Usually groups range from 10-20 people or families. They save regularly, usually in weekly or monthly meetings, into a common fund, with collective decision-making (such decision-making works better in homogeneous communities and not so well in individualistic societies, as trust is an important element for success). They provide collateral-free loans on terms decided by the group at market-driven rates. Millions are being benefitted by these schemes globally.

ROSCA's

A rotating savings and credit association is a form of peer to peer banking and peer to peer lending. It is a poor man or more often woman's bank, where money changes hands rapidly. The group meets weekly or monthly and put in the same amount. One member is given the sum for her needs or business. Every transaction is seen during the meetings, so the transparency and simplicity works well in communities with low levels of literacy. Usually there is a time limit to the group up to six months till al have accessed the fund. Then they may start again.

Debt Banking Model

Banks exist to put people into debt. They make money off debt and interest on that debt.

ASCA's

Accumulating Savings and Credit Savings groups are a little more complicated. Leadership is appointed, at least a chairperson, treasurer. Records are kept and surpluses lent out. As a person receives a loan from the group they must have a business plan and demonstrate that they can repay the loan on a regular basis from the profits of their business. These processes may continue for extended periods of time, so the communal capital grows.

SHG linkages

The church has been at the forefront of implementing Self Help Savings and cooperatives across the world since the early foundation of the World Council of Churches in the 1940's.

More recently, the global banking systems have realised they can make money off such groups. It has become obvious that cooperative savings groups of the poor pay back their loans and are a good banking risk and so there have been international mandates passed down through the national banking systems to bring the poor into the formal banking systems through both these savings groups and other microfinance mechanisms.[9]

This is both good and bad. In Christian savings groups much effort is invested with people to train them in the skills of management and successful business. Banks are only interested in profit, so tend to reduce these services. This means they undercut the costs of operating by the Christian groups that follow a more holistic approach to development. On the other hand, it is good - now, after may decades, the poor are beginning to gain access to the formal economy much more easily.

Self Help Group Bank linkages are programs devised by banks globally to enable these groups to obtain bank accounts and hence demonstrate credit worthiness, then to loan them capital for business formation processes. The poor have no collateral, but their demonstrated discipline in savings provides a firm basis for the banks to advance loans and get them into micro-financing systems. It is to the bank's advantage to facilitate such groups into entrepreneurial success. In India, this has become a national strategy to eliminate poverty.

Mutual Societies and Credit Unions

Mutual Societies and Credit Unions have sprung up in different forms in many countries globally. Some were modelled on mutual societies that developed in England and Europe in the 19th century. These became legalised in the Friendly Societies Acts, and today are found in mutual insurance companies, lodges and Credit Unions in New Zealand.

Since these are mutual, any profits go back each year to the shareholders, who are the members, none are deviated to capital investors. It is interesting to note that in the US during the 2008 crisis, no cooperative banks failed, since being member-driven, they have kept their moneys out of the speculation.

Peer to Peer Capital Formation Networks

More recently a form of peer to peer lending has been emerging, with four companies operating in New Zealand. These cut out the banks to a certain extent, and are based on a certain degree of mutual trust. Thus they are democratising small-scale business lending to some extent.

In a later chapter, we shall examine how these cooperative principles applied to capital formation provide a platform for the emergence of small entrepreneurial businesses

But we have missed one step. To move from capital formation to entrepreneurship, usually one needs to develop capacity to own housing - that in turn provides a basis for access to capital for a small business. So next, we turn to a Biblical theology of land and land ownership and its relationship to the realities of the dream of *the Kiwi half gallon, quarter acre pavlova paradise*. It

79

was a dream of my generation and those past. It's a dream that now has slipped through the fingers of my children's generation.

Liberty Trust: A Vision of Escaping Economic Bondage

One model that breaks the power of debt in New Zealand is *Liberty Trust* — a cooperative venture enabling people to place their money for housing into a common pool, then making no-interest loans from that pool to others, until all in the pool have received sufficient to escape bondage to bank interest. It was born in a vision received by a nurse and then discussed with Bruce MacDonald, a New Life pastor, during the charismatic renewal and has operated since 1985, setting free over 230 families from the banks.

Figure 7: God owns it! But you can be his manager!

8. The Kingdom of God, Land and Ownership

We now turn to developing a Biblical theology around principle 10, ownership – with particular focus on land.[1] This is the foundation of Capitalism. Those societies that have clear land rights and simple processes of adjudication most rapidly utilise the wealth base of society. Capital formation described in the last chapter is not easily done unless one can buy their own home and land.

1.4 billion people in global mega-cities are illegal, living on land not their own - they are known as squatters, landless people, dispossessed twice. First, they have become landless through increased exploitation by the rural rich. For in the process of growing world urbanisation, a growing income differential has been increased between the land-owning wealthy, and the poor. Losing even the little land they have in the rural areas, many flock to the cities where they seek another foothold, a small piece of land on which to build a little shack, a little piece of security. But since the processes of gaining title can take many years, for a second time they are dispossessed of rights, and identified as illegal. In some countries they are thus non-persons.

These are the people among whom, along with some amazing saints, I have lived for long seasons and worked for 40 years. In our struggles for land for squatters, I began to understand my Maori brothers' and my Pakeha ancestors' struggle for land.[2]

A Crucial Pastoral Issue

Land rights is the fundamental pastoral issue for millions in these cities. Without it they have little hope of ever moving out of their squalor and destitution. With it comes the possibilities of home ownership and the dignity this brings to a man and his wife; of jobs created by such housing development and of children growing up in dignity and health.

> *I see the splatter of blood on the walls of a community of squatters in which I once lived. Madame Imelda Marcos sent in the marines to move the people off her son-in-law's land. Two were murdered, seventeen wounded. This tragedy could have been prevented by reasonable talk, responsible consultation, and wise planning for development in this city.*

As a spiritual leader, had I been wiser, perhaps I could have had a role to play in laying a long term web of relationships that would have precluded such bloodshed. Sometimes there are sins of omission that cost lives, making us as guilty as those whose sin leads them to commit murder. This issue of land is one of life and death, and it is one where a faulty theology has led to our non-involvement as Christians. That has led to the countless suffering and poverty and death of millions we could have rescued had we but studied the word of God.

A Crucial Issue for Cultural-Spiritual Revival

Our nation of New Zealand has as one cornerstone in its formation a treaty drafted between the leaders of two peoples, freely entered into by its signatories. Central to the issues of the treaty were a mutually advantageous agreement trading overall sovereignty to the land for protection of land rights.

The identity and *mana* of the Maori people is related to the land and hence to this treaty. To the Maori, this treaty was essentially a covenant with spiritual significance, signed in the context of encouragement from spiritual leaders.

The failure of successive *Pakeha* governments to effectively uphold and honour this treaty in letter and spirit has been perhaps the most significant factor in a sense of lost dignity and caused a long turning away from the gospel by the Maori people after 90% had come Christians in two people movements – an amazing story that Tippett relates in *People Movements in Southern Polynesia*.[3]

The wounded soul of that people echoes the words made to Captain Hobson in April 1840:

> *Our hearts are dark and gloomy from what the Pakeha have told us, they say that the missionaries first came to pave the way for the English who have sent the Governor here, that soldiers will follow and then he will take away our lands.*

The battle for the soul of the Maori people is occurring today. And central to it is reconciliation and restitution over injustices about land rights. If the church fails to be central in this process it fails in its duty as the religious leadership of the nation and leaves options open for a return to the old worship of the demonic and to extreme activists. If the church is central in the process of redressing injustice, it may have the privilege of both strengthening the image of God within the soul of the Maori people and of laying the groundwork for the return of the Maori people to serving the living God.

The Treaty of Waitangi and the Land

The second article of the English text which is attached to the Treaty of Waitangi Act 1975 and which was the version signed at Waikato is as follows:

> *Her Majesty the Queen of England confirms and guarantees to the Chiefs and Tribes of New Zealand and to the respective families and individuals thereof*

> the full exclusive and undisturbed possession of their Lands and Estates Forests
> Fisheries and other properties which they may collectively or individually possess
> so long as it is their wish and desire to retain the same in their possession; but
> the Chiefs of the United Tribes and the individual Chiefs yield to Her Majesty
> the exclusive right of Preemption over such lands as the proprietors thereof may
> be disposed to alienate at such prices as may be agreed upon between the
> respective Proprietors and persons appointed by Her Majesty to treat with them
> in that behalf.

The Theological Context

What are the issues? The right to stay. The right to own. The right to sell The rights of landowners in mega-urban contexts.

In seeking to understand these issues we must oscillate from the realities and traumas of terrible oppression and murder over the land of the poor, to biblical perspectives on the land, the law and the rights of the poor. We can touch on the legal issues involved but will focus on biblical factors related to land.

Land issues are never non-emotive issues of right and wrong. Land is never just dirt but is always dirt in the context of meanings inherited from historical experience.

LAND=DIRT + HISTORY + EMOTION

Land issues can best be studied in the context of five movements in the scriptures related to the land. Each movement has a motif of movement towards a promised land. The first is one of dispossession. The next three movements are followed by possession. The fifth is a movement yet to be fulfilled, a pilgrim people looking forward to a holy city.[4]

We can track from the loss of a garden to the hard work of farming; to Abraham wandering in search of promised land; from slavery in Egypt to the exodus with its promise of land; to its possession and management, and mismanagement resulting in its loss. The story repeats itself finding a promise in the midst of exile, then moves to subsequent repossession of the gifted land. Yet the promise remains unfulfilled, and a Messiah lifts our eyes yet higher to another land to possess. Meanwhile we walk as strangers and pilgrims and exiles on the earth awaiting this blessed hope.

Within these movements there is some puzzlement for pilgrim Christians as to how to identify with the Old Testament attitudes to the land. This is surprising since land is the fourth most frequent noun in the Old Testament

84

(it occurs 2,504 times).[5] The difficulty is because of the lack of focus on land in the New Testament. A development of these themes based on a Kingdom of God perspective, beginning in Genesis, is helpful to clarify the unity of land themes in both testaments.

Brueggemann has integrated his study around themes of landlessness/ landedness, gifted land/grasped land, crucifixion/ resurrection. New Testament studies owe a debt to two excellent studies: Davies, *The Gospel and the Land* primarily related to the question of Jewish land (which I have no intention of addressing here), and Hengel's work, *Property and Riches in the Early Church*. Chris Wright's explorations are currently popular.[6]

These Biblical themes require relating to the global and national conversations and major literature about ecology and some related to developmental issues particularly agricultural land reform. In New Zealand, issues of agricultural and forestry productivity feature high on our success as a nation. As an aside, my father developed national processes in soil science research with the Ministry of Agriculture that upgraded New Zealand's productivity. I remember him reflecting in his later life on his Christian commitment and how he saw that in his facilitating the increase of land productivity in New Zealand by about two billion dollars, he had served God and country well. As a humble Christian scientist without accolade, likely he had never mentioned this to anyone else.

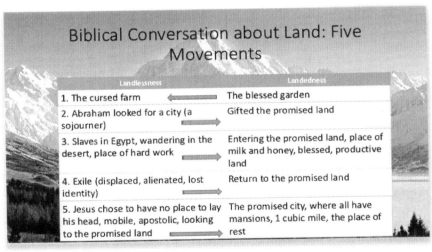

Figure 8: Five movements between landedness and landlessness.

We also face particular issues related to Maori – Pakeha land issues. And over the last two decades has come a *tsumani* of complexities as New Zealand lands have been sold to foreign owners, many with no linkage to the land except for exploitation and profit. How do we interlink the Biblical conversations with these complex issues?

The Nature of Land

Genesis 1-3 contains the seeds of most of the themes of the scriptures, the philosophical perspectives around which the rest of the scriptures expand. Its first verse begins with both the Kingship of God and the relationship of that Kingdom to the land. *In the beginning God created the heavens and the earth...* By virtue of God's creating the land he owns it. Thus in the first verse in the scriptures we have a fundamental statement as to land rights.

The land was created *good*.[7] It was also created *fruitful*.[8] It is through this fruitfulness that real wealth is created, and continues to grow. The total amount of wealth in the world is not static. Nor is it created by increasing paper money. It has a definite growth rate in proportion to the use of natural resources and their replenishment.

But this fruitfulness is directly related to the blessing of God. And that blessing is in some mysterious way related to humanity's obedience to God. Creation was not made independent of humanity. When Adam fell into sin the land was cursed.[9]

Similarly, all of God's covenants with humanity are generally in relationship to the land. The implication is that ministry among the urban poor cannot be effected without attention to the issue of rights to their land - that their knowledge of God is intimately connected with their relationship to the land.

Monetary Realism

The total amount of wealth in the world is not static. Nor is it created by increasing paper money. It has a definite growth rate in proportion to the use of natural resources and their replenishment.

I have seen how, almost overnight, as a community received rights to its land the spiritual environment has been transformed. Men cease gambling and drinking and start investing money into their houses. Women and families gain security and there is a positive thankfulness to God that emerges in the midst of the sound of hammer and concrete mixing.

While God is our final environment, we can only know him in the spatial and temporal forms of his creation.[10]

The Maori relationship to land in New Zealand, as with the relationship of other tribal societies is far more closely akin to this biblical theme than the

Pakeha or other Westernised cultures. To the Maori, this land was not just a commercial asset, but had a spiritual dimension. It was *turangawaewae*, a place to stand, and acknowledgment of identity and status.

These are good things and part of God's mandate to mankind to manage the earth as his vice-regents. The management of these resources through agriculture and manufacturing also results in industry and banking. We may become rich through the wise use of these resources as God's managers, but it is God who made them fruitful. This relationship is not one purely of cause and effect but of a personal creator with his creation. Such thinking denies a core value of the materialistic society. Leviticus 26 is a beautiful chapter showing this interrelationship of God's blessing, mankind's work, and the fruitfulness of the land. Elsewhere we are commanded to:

> *Beware lest you say in your heart 'my power and the might of my hand have gotten me this wealth. You shall remember the Lord your God for it is he who gives you power to get wealth.*[11]

The mystery remains. It was gifted to satisfy, as a good land, a land of bread and honey, of vineyards and trees, cities and houses, and cisterns of water.[12] This was in contrast with the demanding land of Egypt, the land of effort with no reward, the land of coercion and slavery. The difference was the blessing and grace of God.

This fruitfulness of the land, and its inherent goodness is disordered as a result of the rebellion and fall but there is no evidence that this essential goodness is destroyed. Moreover, creation is not created to stand still, but to develop and grow. In fact, one could say that though creation is good, part of its goodness lies in what it can become, in the process that God has initiated.[13]

Mankind then, is to manage this land and its fruitfulness on God's behalf for the well-being of their brothers and sisters, for from the outset the cry of "Am I my brother's keeper?" refuses to remain silent as it echoes from the hills and valleys of history. The land is not independent from issues of social responsibility. It is from the land that his brother's blood cries out its reply.

Promised Land

When we meet Israel, it is a nation without land on the way to a promised land. A landless folk and a land of promise. The patriarchs are known as sojourners who are looking for a land. This is the focus of their faith.

Sojourner is a technical word usually described as a *resident alien*. It means to be in a place, perhaps for an extended time, to live there and take some roots, but always to be an outsider, never belonging, always without rights, title or voice in decisions that matter.[14]

Abraham, renowned because of always looking for a city yet only seeing it afar off, finds a land, sojourns in it, but dwells content that he has an heir to bring about the fulfilment of the promise of possession. Abraham could be called the first squatter. For the fulfilment took place by degrees. We find Jacob his son, as he is about to die, asking that his body be carried to the promised land[15] recognizing a promise given yet unfulfilled.

So too, for the one billion migrants to the cities of the third world these last thirty years, possession has been by degrees. They too look for a city as a centre of hope, and little by little find their foothold, often content to know that though they themselves dwell in miserable poverty, their children will possess the land of promise.

In their case, the promise is not a covenant from God. Or is it? Is there inherent within the nature of the God-man-land relationship a fundamental law that all men are entitled to a plot of land for a house? Is it inherent within the nature of man's relationship to man, woman's relationship to woman, that some land be apportioned for every person and their basic needs be catered for?

> **Graced Economics**
>
> We are to manage on God's behalf, but that management is not sufficient for fruitfulness. There is an element of grace, an element of giftedness, an element of undeserved blessing. Similarly, we find the land gifted to Israel.

It is generally recognised by governments as a basic right for a family to own his own piece of land for a home and be able to obtain the basic necessities of life. As such, might we not say it is promised by God? Not promised with exact boundaries and area and geographical precision, nor with a now time frame. But then neither was Abraham's hope fixed with clear boundaries and his time frame was determined through the dark brooding of a prophetic dream about four hundred years of slavery.

The hope of Abraham was not based on any right he had to the land. Other tribes already had laid claim to it. The land would be his because it was gifted by God to him. Thirty-nine times in Deuteronomy assertions about the land as gift occur.[16]

So too for the squatters. Due to colonial policies of land exploitation in most countries, a few families own the land in each city. Any change in this legalised oppression will only appear to the poor that the Lord has given them the land as a gift.

The initiative is with God, so we need to encourage our people to fall on their knees before God and seek this blessing. For this they can freely ask since the goodness of such a gift is inherent in his being, in his own creative relationship to mankind and creation, in his purposes for the dignity of man and woman.

Yet such prayer does not mean a passive inactivity concerning obtaining legal rights. There are many factors to be considered as a basis for land rights. These occur in many societies, urban and rural.

The land is beyond Israel's power to acquire. The defeats of Kadesh-Barnea and Ai are sufficient evidence of this. This does not mean they sit back and do nothing. Preparations are made, battles are engaged. But it is God who directs and who gives victory. So too the squatters need leadership developed, and need to learn the techniques required for success in the struggles for land rights. But it is God who is the giver of the land.

Ownership and Management of the Land

Israel was not only sojourner, there were long periods where they were landed people. The sojourners become possessors.

God Owns the Land

> **Which Basis for Ownership Claims?**
>
> *Paptipu* - right of discovery
> *Take tuku* - a gift
> *Rapatu* - right of conquest
> *Ahi-ka roa* - long occupation
> *Take tupuna* - kinship ties.

Before their entrance into the land, Moses pauses and gives instructions about the land. Many of the principles related to the land are given in the teaching on the Jubilee in Lev 25:8-34.

In the midst of it we find that God owns the land. Hence men are only to be God's tenants on the land, God's stewards or managers on his behalf, free to share in the fruits of his crops but answerable to him. He is the title-holder.

Private, Family, Clan and Tribal Ownership

Joshua apportions to each clan and each family of Israelites a portion of land, a family inheritance.[17] This indicates God's blessing on both private and family/clan/tribal ownership of the land (where we are using ownership in the common sense of the word, recognizing that ultimately God owns the land).

Maori tribal and clan structure is anthropologically in the same category as the Israelites of this period. The land belongs to the tribe (*iwi*) and was well defined. There was no such thing as unused, ownerless land, merely different forms of land use. The *hapu* (sub-tribe, clan), the *whanau* (extended family) and the individual might have hereditary rights to its use, but ownership was ultimately vested in the iwi. This differs from the tribal and clan structure of Israel where both communal and family land rights were recognised. The difference is cultural. The Biblical principles involved are an affirmation of both communal and individual ownership patterns within a tribal or rural society.

It also differs from the Maori understanding when the Pakeha arrived for the concept of land as a commodity which could be exploited through resale was new to the Maori. With the exception of the speculative purchases just before 1840, Maori land had usually been alienated to secure the benefits of the Pakeha presence... It was clear however that Maori accepted the concept of total alienation of land rights through sale only after considerable experience.[18]

The titles court of 1862 and the Maori Land Court Act of 1865 in New Zealand essentially violated these principles. The court was bound by a statute to name no more than ten owners to a piece of land, with the result that the rest were dispossessed by ten. It took away the authority of the elders so that decision-making was in the hands of the courts and lawyers.

The scriptures are consistently strong on maintenance of legal boundaries. Deut 19:14 and other passages tell us what many government officials need to learn - never to remove the ancient boundary pegs. If we do, their Redeemer is strong; he will plead their case against us.[19] We need to respect private and communal property rights.

Today Pakeha believers in New Zealand are involved in redressing this situation and effecting restitution. If you read the Waitangi tribunals introduction to its report on Orakei *marae* you will find an excellent analysis of the injustices that occurred to this tribe concerning their land through the last century and adjudication of responsibility, analysis of what restitution is needed and what is practical.

Restitution in most situations in life cannot be exact, for acts of evil carry consequences that are irreversible. Time moves on. Restitution needs to be symbolic and real in terms of present economic realities which for the Orakei *marae* involved the equivalent of what the land used to mean - resources for economic life for the youth of the tribe.

Limitations to Private Ownership

But God is not a capitalist, nor is he a communist. Ownership is not unlimited nor absolute. Nor is ownership to be invested in the state alone. Private ownership has validity but it is bounded by the needs of others to use the earth's resources.

In the Jubilee which occurred every fifty years this land was to be given freely back to these original owners so that the development of social classes through a few men gaining control of much property could not occur. God does not want society to be polarised into rich landowners and landless peasants, where "the rich get richer" and "the poor get poorer."

The Bible teaches both private ownership and related social responsibility. It recognises both the need for human freedom and the controls that need to be placed on the free exercise of human evil.

The Lord gave the command that the land lie fallow every seventh year. This is an initial principle that has been interpolated into the theory of ecology. Exploitation and destruction of lands and foliage is a violation of our roles as "stewards" and "managers". This "rest" is also talked of when they were considering entering the promised land. it was to be a land of promised rest. Rest from harassment, from enemies, from sojourning, a place called home, a place of physical security. How much the squatters need a place of such rest. The psychological stresses of living under plywood and galvanised iron, with rats nightly visiting and garbage uncollected next door cause the poor to cry out for rest. How they need the rest of freedom from harassment by landowners and politicians.

Religious priests also were to have their own home and a plot of land sufficient for family food but not fields. This was in the context of God being their possession. The implication is that pastors and missionaries today while looking to God to provide their needs are within the framework of scriptures to look to God for a modest home also.

Ownership Limited by Social Responsibility

Forest lands, oil lands, mining lands among others are so critical to the needs of total societies that absolute rights to these and capitalistic exploitation is not beneficial to the good of the country as a whole. Such are contrary to the principle of social responsibility.

But are we correct to blithely apply these principles to our day? What differences in the practices outlined here are demanded today as we interpret the scriptures into a mega-urban society in secular semi-capitalist states? Certainly the fifty years of the Jubilee would not be enforceable. And yet it brings up two principles: periodic land reform in third world societies as they seek an equitable redistribution of the imbalances of colonial exploitation and the necessity for economic reform within the capitalist system. Continuous economic growth without planned periodic redistribution is not part of God's program for society.

Related to this jubilee we may infer that cancelling of debts and liberating slaves are both insufficient acts in agrarian contexts if they are not correlated with return of land - the means of production of wealth. Perhaps this was part of the failure of the American civil war. It appears that any revolutionary government must immediately move to land reform as its primary act of governance if justice fought for is to be seen done.

Urban Land

In the city the production of wealth is built on a different foundation. Notice Moses' clear differentiation between agricultural lands and urban land. Houses within cities were not to be subject to redistribution. After a year during which they could be redeemed, they could then be sold in perpetuity. The meaning of land in the city is clearly different to the meaning of land in the countryside. For in the country the land is seen as representative of the fruit of that land, and measured in worth according to the number of crops before the next jubilee. The land in the city had no such relationship per se to the production of wealth.

So too for the Maori people today they cannot go back to the old times for history has urbanised. The meaning of the land has changed. And the treaty left the relationships between the races open to continual growth and development.

The question for our day thus becomes "What is the meaning of land in the city?" and "In what way can that meaning be related to just and equitable earnings and distribution of wealth?"

The answer does not necessarily coincide with legal definitions of land rights. Legality does not mean morality. We stand before a set of higher laws than the laws of nations, made often by rich elites with entrenched interests in maintaining control of land.

The question is one of justice with equity not just of legality.

The questions are necessary questions for societies other than Israel that have many migrant populations. Migration does not lend itself to the static allocation of land demonstrated in the early agrarian days of Israel. Increasing movement and ethnic interrelationships require different definitions and uses of land.

A further troublesome issue when we consider this issue of social equity in regard to use of urban land is the conflict between the clarity within the scriptures of God's commitment to relative equality between men (that we are not to Lord it over each other, that kings were not a class above the people but representatives of the people and God's representative to the people), and the sociological reality that cities apparently exist by exploitation and inequality.

Even the story of the glory of the Kingdom under Solomon is an illustration of the rapid stratification of society as a correlate of urbanisation. The commitment of God against class structure (inherent in James' teaching for example), coupled with his commitment to urbanisation per se, as the direction of history would indicate that urbanisation without stratification is a possibility and a worthy goal. Social equality is not a realistic possibility in a city unless the majority of people can freely own their own homes.

Economic justice, social justice and accessible land rights are inextricably linked to godliness, to bringing righteousness into urbanisation.

The opposite is generally the case. We can go back to the scriptures to see a case study in injustice that is echoed throughout the earth. The land of promise soon became the land of problem. Guaranteed satiation dulls the memory of the voice of God that has led them to this land and gifted it to them. The covenant that is part of the gifting is soon forgotten. Kings and the upper class soon turned it into a land of oppression and slavery as predicted by the prophet Samuel. Israel tried frantically to hold on to the land against outside enemies. As the society developed into a commercial urban society under the hands of Solomon and his sons, the jubilee was evidently not maintained. The rich became richer; the poor became poorer. It became a coercive society where:

> *The ones who have made it, the ones who control the machinery of governance are the ones who need not so vigorously obey. They are the ones who can fix tickets or prices as needed, the ones before whom the judge blinks and the revenue officer winks (cf. Micah 3:11). It is the landless poor and disadvantaged who are subject to exacting legal claims of careful money management, precise work performance, careful devotion to all social jots and tittles, not only the last hired, and first fired but first suspected and last acquitted.[20]*

The people soon forgot that fulfilled covenantal responsibility is integral to land tenure. Harlotry and shedding of blood defile the land.[21] Blessing follows obedience, cursing and deportation follows disobedience.[22] The gift, the tenancy agreement, had conditions then and for the poor today the conditions remain.

> **Urban Stratification**
>
> As the society developed into a commercial urban society under the hands of Solomon, the rich became richer, the poor became poorer. It became a coercive society.

The Prophet's Critique of Land Owners

Into this arena step the prophets with bold denunciation of those who trample on the poor to acquire more and more property:

> *Woe to those who join house to house,*
> *who add field to field,*
> *until there is no more room,*
> *and you are made to dwell alone*
> *in the midst of the land.*[23]

> *They covet fields, and seize them;*
> *and houses and take them away;*
> *they oppress a man and his house,*
> *a man and his inheritance.*[24]

It is from these kind of prophetic statements that we find an emotive imperative for defending the squatters against the exploitation and attacks of the upper class.

The prophets both denounce such acts and cry out for men of God who would protect these poor. They denounce creditors who foreclosed mortgaged houses and fields, and high officials who confiscated more crown lands than the king had given them, exorbitant interest rates on loans which led to quick and cruel foreclosure, resulting in self-enslavement and enclosure of property.[25]

The prophets denounced those who refused to care for the poor, the widows, the orphans, the sojourner, the Levite - all of whom did not possess land. In a peasant society, a man without land is subject to poverty for it is the land that produces wealth. Thus the landless must be cared for, and the poor must be protected from those who would make them yet poorer by stealing (legally of course), their land.

Today, owing to destruction of farmlands, warfare, overpopulation, and the tentacles of urbanisation and stratification as they reach out to exploit the countryside, there is a growing class of hundreds of millions of permanently dispossessed, landless people. Though our vision may only become fulfilled in that holy city, we must struggle for a reallocation of the land to these poor.

The extent of land ownership makes for the extent of justice in a society. Though this is defined in the scriptures in the context of a peasant society and rural land holdings it is not inaccurate to restate this for the urban societies of today. In an urban context the extent of injustice within a city is proportional to the number of people who rent homes or rooms.

This statement implies something about the nature of urban land. It implies the right to housing. The effort to bring this to pass conflicts however with the utilisation of land in the city as a commodity. Land is seen to have an intrinsic value not for its fruitfulness (as in agrarian societies), nor for housing. but for its usefulness to the production of wealth.

Thus one role of leadership within a society is to make ways for equitable distribution of land and ownership. Yet that has to be done within the framework of the specialisations of production and distribution and their implication for land values that are endemic to the modern mega-city.

Exile: The Loss of a Land

The Sabbath and the land are quite closely intertwined in the Old Testament covenants. The prophets denounced the breaking of the Sabbath - for a Sabbath less society reduces the nation to a smoothly functioning machine and thus its people to cogs within that machine. The machine raises a producer - consumer consciousness that denies the image of God as the core of a person's being. The Sabbath on the other hand sets limits to our most frantic efforts to manage life - it is a way of remembering that we are the creature, not the ruler.

In judgment on these sins of Sabbath-breaking, of injustice, of loss of role before him, before other men and before the land, he takes away their land, the symbol of the covenant. The great themes of the exile relate to the loss of the land. And a question of despair echoes through their songs and laments. Does loss of the land of covenant mean loss of the God of the covenant?

Return from Exile

Even in this process there is a renewed covenant that they will return to the land. And beyond the covenant are glimpses of a far greater covenant, and of a city to be seen only with the faith of their forefather Abraham.

In the return from exile the new covenant concerning the land is made.[26] This covenant is now based on a new moral management of the land.

It is this thrill of return to the promised land that we can best relate to the task of working for squatter land rights in the two thirds world, for migrant housing, for expansion of low income housing in New Zealand. Nehemiah is perhaps the best model for mobilizing a people to action. His experience and that of Ezra and the other prophets of this period deal with the fears, the uncertainties, the group dynamics, the leadership skills needed as people dispossessed of their rural land seek to possess unused urban areas.

But even in the return to the land there is no dramatic development in the Israelites' walk with God. So finally prophecy ceases from the land. The land waits. Creation awaits the coming of the Word and in his new promise waits even longer for the fulfilment of time.

Jesus and the Land

With Jesus' mission, a dramatic new relation to the land is evident.[27]

A major issue for theologians is the lack of continuity of the Old Testament with issues of land in the New Testament. The Old Testament covenant regarding the land of Israel is now superseded with a new covenant which looks forward to a new land of promise that is not bounded by ethnic concerns - a land for every tribe and people and tongue. The themes of the exodus and exile are reiterated with renewed vigour. Again, believers find themselves as pilgrim people living by a promise, *looking forward to a heavenly city whose builder and maker is God*. In the process many are encouraged to follow the master who chose to have *no place to lay his head* in order that he might proclaim this far-off country.

Does this mean a loss of commitment to the principles of management and social responsibility in the Old Covenant? Not in the least. The old was not abrogated. It was fulfilled and expanded to include the nations of the earth in fuller realisation. Precisely because we are exiles and pilgrims with no possessions of our own we are able to help the dispossessed to gain their possession. In our looking towards a future Kingdom, we are eager to pray and act towards that Kingdom being manifest in every way within the societies of earth. And that future Kingdom comes replete with a promise of a home - something every squatter and migrant and dispossessed person understands.

We must go forward to that promise. And in the process we must bring to fulfilment the promises of God to the poor. Promises that wherever the kingdom flourishes they will possess the land that is their birthright stolen during colonialization. Land that can only be returned as a gift from God. In the process we may frequently fail but always because our eyes are fixed on a future Kingdom, we are free to bring hope, free to proclaim a more glorious home - one not built with hands, one that will not disappear or fade away. Let us go on to proclaim that hope in the midst of sharing in the struggles of our brother poor.

All of this conversation between scriptures and land rights was not too complicated to imagine when New Zealand was a sovereign nation. But as $27 billion of the nation's government assets have been sold off over the last years, applying the same principles to the internationalisation process is a significantly more complex set of issues. We turn to such issues in the latter half of this book.

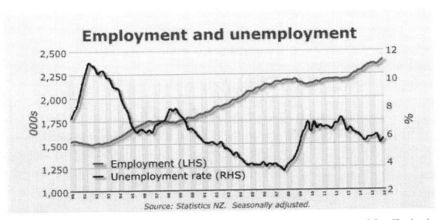

Figure 9: The Economic Conversation is sourced with multiple layers of data in New Zealand, indicating reasonable health.

Part 3: Discipleship of Economic Systems

The third, the theological reflection of Part 2 that integrated some of the Biblical themes into a *Biblical theology*.

We now turn in step four, to the social analysis or in this case, the *economic conversation*.

This leads to the final integration of the issues, the theological themes and the economic themes into a framework for *transformational conversation*.

Economist Talk

Most of us have to admit that economists, to us, are a special kind of geek, who speak in gracious phrases, with English words, but in a language all of their own (No offence meant to our learned friends!!). We generally have difficulty with bills designed by accountants where numbers and columns always appear with negatives when they mean positives and vice versa. Their English words tell us we are in serious legal trouble for whatever we ought to have done that we have not done, but which is not evident in the bill. Economists add to that way of thinking a complete layer of philosophic language that is always measured and explains that if something went up, something must come down, but all things go round. .

So how can we have any kind of theological conversation?

First, they begin with some presuppositions that to them are as central as the scriptures are to Christians, but which seem far removed from our realities. If we don't grasp those, then we might be talking at cross purposes! Economics 101 doesn't help most of us as the mathematical constructs become daunting. I was able to grasp some of these when I found a good comic book explaining *Economix*. [1] At a more serious level (but still with pictures), *O Livro da Economia* [2] became one book I used to improve my Portuguese, my wife's mother tongue. R.H. Tawney, early last century updated many of Adam Smith's ideas and their relationship to Christianity. Renowned sociologist, Peter Berger, in his *Fifty Propositions about Capitalism*, is a most lucid writer on Capitalism.

Key Economic Theoretical Constructs

It is helpful to look at a few foundational premises. Frank Scrimgeour [3] in some notes on *Economics, Faith and the 21st Century* identifies some elements underlying economist's thinking.

First, economic analysis highlights the observation that **economic outcomes are the results of choice and preference.** I may *prefer* apples – you may *prefer* bananas; I may *prefer* to spend more on health – you may *prefer* to spend more on education; I may *prefer* to spend more on controlling greenhouse gas emissions – you may *prefer* to spend more on reducing nitrogen contamination in waterways. These preferences may be informed to some degree by ethical convictions.

Second, **the laws of supply and demand** characterize the behaviour of people, firms, institutions and organizations. Producers face opportunity costs when seeking to increase production, and higher prices do generate a supply response. Consumers demonstrate a declining marginal willingness to pay for goods and services. The interaction of supply and demand determines the quantities and prices of goods and services, which move in predictable ways in response to changes in supply and demand.

Third, there are many **economic agents making decisions**. Individuals make decisions as members of households, as employees, managers, consumers, voters and investors. It is critical that policy advocates and policy makers recognize the participation of the all agents in the economy.

Fourth, if we ignore **externalities and time**, we may miss the most important consequences of a particular choice. Consumption constraints today may cause higher or lower consumption in future. External effects not represented in market prices may be significant, perhaps even larger than market returns.

Fifth, **economic governance** arrangements are important. Constitutional arrangements governing the Reserve Bank are arguably more important than the Bank's decisions. Similarly company law and employment law are major determinants of economic outcomes and the associated transaction costs of achieving these outcomes. Christians should **focus on institutional design** and the sets of decisions facing a company or council or government as opposed to considering each concern in isolation.

With the fourth and fifth principles particularly in mind, we may tentatively examine some New Zealand structural issues of our times.

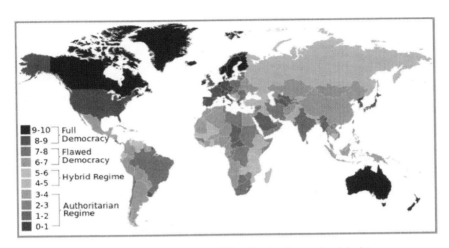

Figure 10: *Openness of governance. New Zealand tops the global transparency ranking.*[1]

9. Biblical Principles & Political Economy

Jesus calls us to disciple the nations – to bring not just the people but the structures and the culture under his authority. Thus economic discipleship for those who have leadership roles in society or the church requires critiquing, changing, modifying, opposing the prevailing economic philosophies and powers, as we both bring the Kingdom and wrestle against the spiritualities and powers that oppress our society.

The first step in a *Transformational Conversation* for a nation is identifying the pain of dissonance, the discontinuities, the chaos.

The second step, is the Biblical reflections in different periods of Redemptive history in Part 1.

The third step in Part 2 has been to reflect on some issues form these Biblical Theologies.

In part 3 we reverse that process, reflecting from some national issues back to the scriptures, then looking at the action and structural outcomes to bring about Societal Transformation

We cannot grapple with the Kingdom and society without venturing into macro-economics, the economics of the structures of society, of aggregate groups of people within a society or between societies. Recently we have seen the emergence of a right-wing Republican style Christianity in the U.S. espousing extreme versions of Capitalism. A decade before that we have had Latin Americans espousing a baptised version of Marxism in Liberation Theology. In the Biblical tradition, both the classic Catholic tradition along with the mainline Protestant tradition has been critical of both Marxism and Capitalism, and have consistently spoken of *a third way* based on enabling cooperative versions of free enterprise within the framework of some forms of communal redistribution of wealth.

All of these are an important framing of a debate about the end goals of economics. But end goals are the heart of Christian ethical reflection. The Greek classical tradition calls it the *Common Good*. For Christians, the Kingdom of God defines that common good. Rauschenbush in 1916, wrote

> The Kingdom of God defines the common good, the highest and the best.

a theology of social and economic thought where the Kingdom of God was defined as the highest good. It became the source of liberal theological social agendas for the next century. While his conversion of that into a systems approach became problematic, the truth stands.

The following expand some of the themes we developed in the previous chapters related to (1) individual, (2) family and (3) local community finances. These are now developed into a conversation between theological principles applied to the ethics of macro-economics at (4) national and (5) global levels. Given the complexity of macro-economic structures, such a short study can only be introductory, suggestive. Given that most of us will not become economists that is appropriate. We need to understand enough to be able to converse the gospel with the professionals, but they need to implement that gospel within their disciplines.

Liberty and Limitations to Government

There are limits to the ruling of humanity over other humans that derive from the first chapter of the scriptures. In them is defined a fundamentally different relationship between man and man, woman and woman to that of men and women to creation. The emphasis of our relationship to creation is an emphasis of management, rulership, as vice-regents, in the same manner as the Governor-General of New Zealand represents the interests of the British Crown in New Zealand. The emphasis of our social relationships is that of care, brotherhood, equality, justice.

Because we are born in his image, each person has an immortal soul and a conscience. Each person is accountable to God to be his brother's keeper. Thus, we are to develop societies that care for each one, protecting the image of God in each one, being accountable for all around us. This is love. We are to create loving societies.

During the dispute between the prophet Samuel and the people about importing the style of a Monarchy into the relatively democratic system of judges and tribes - the theocracy - in 1 & 2 Samuel, we find the prophet speaking of the dangers of centralisation of power around a monarchy, of the oppression by the monarch of the people, of the potential to enslave the people, of the increased taxation. There is a critical principle here of the diffusion of power to the people. A people is as strong as its small organisations at its base - be they small economic units, small political units, or networks of religious societies. These diffuse power and enable processes for emergence of leadership that understands the people's issues.

This is a principle violated by both Capitalism and Socialism. Across Western Capitalist nations over the last 60 years, increasing levels of taxation have fuelled growth of the governmental money supplies and taxation has risen from 5% to over 40% for most OECD countries, increasingly centralising power away from local communities. This requires resistance, a discipleship that stands against these powers, as Jesus stood against the abuses of merchandise in the temple.

Similarly the centralizing of power in multinationals (that are accountable to none except their boards and shareholders, and rarely have significant accountability as to local community consequences of their actions on the environment), is an ongoing violation of this principle that requires prophetic resistance, an unmasking and standing against these powers.

Limits to Sin: The Need for Regulation

The sinfulness of individuals is multiplied in larger societal contexts. Urban communities magnify certain sins. The development in Leviticus and Exodus of various legal structures indicates processes for godly limitations, for punishment of crime. Effective feedback loops, and rapid responses to issues in contexts without corruption are essential. When systems evolve with incremental regulatory changes to deal with changing dynamics, nations are

> ### Diffusion of Power
>
> A people is as strong as the small organizations at its base - be they small economic units, small political units, or networks of religious societies.

healthy. When there is easy feedback from people to legislators, and diffused power within societies, responses to issues can be rapid, hence the society moves forward in an integrated manner.

Efficient bureaucracy or good governance is recognised to advance national economies. Significant levels of governmental management have been critical to the efficiency of first world countries. But overly excessive bureaucratisation is a significant factor in sustaining poverty and dualism within societies. It is considered by de Soto[2] as the direct cause of sustained poverty in many Latin countries that were still emerging from mercantilism till three decades ago, for example.

In New Zealand, we now rank first in terms of our institutional efficiency and fourth in terms of health and educational institutions globally, based on criteria heavily influenced by American perceptions of efficiency. But following the model of over-bureaucratisation due to excessive litigation of the US, the 2016 Proposed Free trade agreement will also bring the intrusion of American lawyers and hence greatly expand the bureaucratisation and legalisation of New Zealand society. This will likely drop New Zealand from being the eighteenth most competitive society in the world.[3]

Limits to Sin: Limits to Government Power

New Zealand has faced a rapid erosion of checks and balances that sustain governmental accountability in the last decades, beginning with the elimination of the upper house of Parliament. This is evidenced in the consistent refusal by governments to listen to the voice of the people in referenda (Helen Clarke's government listened to no referenda that was Christian in derivation), and in the rapid swings between conflicting governing and economic strategies that incoming New Zealand governments have imposed on the people without consent.

Rogernomics was such a swing towards the right, seeking to minimise government involvement, reduce bureaucratisation, eliminate complex compliance costs. It did so, however, without significant concern for serious social costs involved in the rapid process of change. Similarly, Helen Clark's Socialism, its goals defined 30 years earlier, and honed by international socialist values sought to expand bureaucracies, and among other things entered deeply into family liberties based on the socialist value of State-controlled family dynamics and child raising.

It made no apology for increasing levels of taxation in New Zealand to the fourth highest in the OECD, even when there were regular surpluses, and had no compunction about distributing some of these to the middle class, not because of poverty, but because of the consistent Socialist belief in the government as the redistributor of wealth. It overly committed to free trade - particularly opening the doors to free trade with China, prior to China floating its currency at realistic levels. This crashed sectors of New Zealand's economy – clothing production and shoe manufacturing to name two. Perhaps these were sunset industries that could never continue to compete globally. Perhaps workers could have been retrained. Schemes were developed but have not worked in any countries. As industries are lost there is an overall loss of employment, though the theories predict movement to higher level industries, few can make the transitions.

Globally, there has been a rapid increase of centralised bureaucracies in both capitalist and communist societies. With increasing urbanisation and the growth of computerised control technology all countries have some form of central planning. This has clearly been an asset throughout the 20th Century in the abolition of poverty and redistribution of wealth. But the scriptural warning to limit such governmental powers has largely been lost. In OECD countries taxation rises yearly, and is now often over 40% of peoples' income. Along with that, the increase of bureaucratisation is immense. Helen Clark's government added thousands of bureaucrats, and increased the percentage of taxation by 8% over 9 years of power. As in Egypt, the people begin to groan under such burdens. Christians have consistently called for limitations to governmental controls.

Civil and Religious Freedom from Oppression

Our principle ten, *freedom and celebration* has been the basis for Christian opposition to governmental oppression globally for two millennia. There is a poem where one of my Baptist forbears, a certain Gryg, is named as a leader of a march from Kent to London to obtain freedom from the current oppression of his day. My grandfather on another side, because of religious beliefs was imprisoned as a pacifist for opposing engagement in the First World War. On the other side, my grandmother fought for seventy years to free New Zealand from its drunkenness as secretary of the Woman's Christian Temperance Union. Liberty is known as the supreme end to democracy. Something that some of our Bible-believing forebears in England fought for with their blood. Freedom to worship, freedom from oppression is a constant fight for citizens.

Such liberty is fundamental to economic development. Successful wealth formation occurs in contexts of integrity, where trust in contracts, the rule of law, and supportive governmental structures is possible. Capitalism is built on such economic freedom.

Every piece of corruption, of skirting the law, of creating environments of distrust, of creating legalised oppression, drag effective economies down, slowing wealth generation and siphoning wealth off from productive ends.

Principle of Freedom: Government Transparency

How does one measure freedom in today's global context? And how does that match the Biblical vision of liberty and *shalom*?

The flip side of the limitations on government is to look at their openness, transparency and to measure the extent of freedom for engagement in democracy. In 2015, New Zealand ranked first in such a global survey.[4]

This perhaps is the end result of the debacle when Prime Minister Muldoon was unwilling to open the books to Labour in 1983, between the election results and formal transfer of power. *We decided there and then that no new government would ever face this situation again. There would be more openness...Budget forecasts were changed to make debt needs transparent.*[5]

In 2016, New Zealand also ranks third in the World in an *Index of Economic Freedom*, published by the Heritage Foundation. Their index covers the following as measurements of freedom:

Rule of Law

- Property Rights: Degree of a country's legal protection of private property rights, degree of enforcement of those laws, independence of and corruption within the judiciary, and likelihood of expropriation.

- Freedom from Corruption. The non-prevalence of political corruption within a country, according to the *Corruption Perceptions Index* (New Zealand ranks fourth on this index, by Transparency International).

Limited Government

- Fiscal Freedom: How free is a country from tax burden. It comprises three quantitative measures: top marginal tax rate of both individual (1) and corporate (2) income, and total tax burden as a percentage of GDP (3).
- Government Size/Spending: Governments' expenditures as a percentage of GDP, including consumption and transfers. The higher the percent spending, the lower the score.

Regulatory Efficiency

- Business Freedom: A country's freedom from the burden of regulations on starting, operating, and closing business, given factors such as time, cost and number of procedures, as well as the efficiency of government in the regulatory process.
- Labour Freedom: How free is a country from legal regulation on the labour market, including those relating to minimum wages, hiring and firing, hours of work and severance requirements.
- Monetary Freedom: How free from microeconomic intervention and price instability is a country, basing on an equation considering the weighted average inflation rate in the last three years and price controls.

Open Markets

- Trade Freedom: Freedom from sizeable numbers and burdens of tariffs and non-tariff barriers to imports and exports of a country.
- Investment Freedom: Freedom from restrictions on the movement and use of investment capital, regardless of activity, within and across the country's borders.
- Financial Freedom: A country's independence from government control and interference in the financial sector, including banks. It considers government ownership of financial firms, extent of

financial and capital market development, government influence on the allocation of credit and openness to foreign competition.

There is a basis for the above. Historically cities flourish to the degree they possessed economic fluidity and institutional adaptiveness created by economic freedom.[6] At the same time, it is evident that this list has an anti-labour bias and an anti-government intervention bias. The heritage Foundation is known as a right wing foundation.

Liberty and Governmental Redistribution

Shalom is a biblical concept of overall well-being within a nation or people. While we can measure the economic well-being of a country by its GDP, we need to also evaluate the distribution of that wealth in meeting basic human needs, providing a foundation for well-being and opportunities for its people. Again New Zealand comes out as 5th in the Social Progress index which ranks countries on meeting basic human needs; providing a foundation of well-being; creating opportunity for all through personal rights, freedoms, tolerance and inclusion, access to education. Thus the human development index integrates measures of life expectancy, expected years of schooling, as well as income. New Zealand consistently ranks high on this index, excluding income, New Zealand stands as ninth.[7]

Significant as a foundation for this is the social welfare system of a country. Until the early 1800's in England, the local church was responsible for the poor of its parish. As the feudalism of Christendom increasingly broke down, responsibility began to shift to the Government to care for the poor. This became formalised in the 1930's with increasing redistribution by the Welfare State.

There are problems moving from spiritual leadership to power politics. This process lead to removal of another limitation to the power of the Government, with concomitant loss of human liberty (hence of economy). We joke that for many New Zealanders, it has meant that the Government becomes the repository of faith, the solver of all problems! Or is that a lament for a lost national soul??

There are problems with governments taking from the rich and giving to the poor. It imperils political liberty, discourages productivity and disassociates the wealth from those with the knowledge of investment and entrepreneurial knowledge which are keys to economic growth.

There are also problems of distributing to the poor. There are always stories of "scammers", and it would be wrong to glorify the poor as noble or competent as there are many lazy and indolent, and many who are poor

110

because of inability to manage. The distribution system also tends to promote a view of the producers of wealth as the enemy, indeed a violent diabolizing of Capitalism.

It can leave the working poor with little motivation, as often if they attempt part-time work they earn little more than the dole. In that sense it can enfeeble the poor in their struggles to exit poverty, so the rich tell us, though I have yet to see research that verifies this except in isolated anecdotes.

Our New Zealand Social Welfare is efficient, largely effective and has over the years faced and researched all of these issues, to end up at a point of fine balance in creating a safety net at the bottom of society.

Redistribution by the Church as an alternative would be based on effective diaconal development. In today's world, deacons are equivalent to social workers, or economic development experts, or budgeting managers. Yet how many churches have highly trained social workers, budgeting managers on their staff to handle these needs? We are unprepared for the future. By default, much of the New Zealand church has left these roles to WINZ (Work and Income). On the other hand, within the denominations there are significant social service networks, such as the Baptist Oasis, the Salvation Army Social Services. These deliver much of the governmentally funded services to the community. Why? Because of a motivation of care within the churches.

It may be, that post-Capitalism, post-welfare state, such church-based delivery will enable the sustenance of much of the nation. In the meantime, we live with the tension of a secular government, interfaced with the faith community that has the commitment and committed manpower to engage in mitigating the social injustices and engage the needs of the lower economic sectors of society.

Equality and Equity

There are also problems with definitions. Is redistribution more Christian than production? Some also equate distribution with compassion and production with exploitation.

And what is the goal of redistribution? Can we all live at the same level? Surely a family of eleven requires more than a couple. We see in the Acts 2 account that God didn't intend exact equality but he did intend justice and levels that are considered comparatively equal, free and creative. His desire is perhaps best described as equity – not exact equality but a balancing within a range that is seen to be just redistribution.

Production with Social Responsibility

> *Economy itself is the creation and production of value. Since at its root, value is an expression of spiritual qualities with moral implications, religion which is the promulgation of values, is intimately connected to the economy. From this perspective religion can be seen as supply-side in nature...true economy becomes the active expression of God-derived qualities in human endeavour, including the process by which we give raw matter value and purpose and turn it into economic "goods".*[8]

The Gospel creates a new productive system as new communities emerge. This has been reinforced in my thinking as I grapple with how the slums generate their own economic systems. A continual influx of people creates new wealth, new markets. Similarly, as a church develops, there is an increasing amount of resources set free for the Kingdom, and a small economic system develops (unless the church invests too heavily or prematurely in buildings or pastoral staff).

Part of the original *Lifestyle and Values of Servants* as we set up a mission among the poor said this:

> *We will seek to uplift the economy of the poor by working where possible to get the skills to produce the means of production and control of production into the hands of the labouring poor. This involves assisting those in the richer nations or classes in transferral of technology, tools of production, and initiating capital to the poor. We will encourage the development of cooperatives , home-based industries, and vocational training. Our intended model is development from within communities based on existing and developing values, skills and motivations of the poor, rather than large-scale externally imposed projects.*[9]

Those statements remain as guides to lifelong progressions thirty-five years later. And they reflect broader Christian theological commitments to pressure governments to a process of encouraging productivity that engages the poorest and benefits the poorest through their work.

The Biblical statement of reality that *the poor you will have with you always*, linked to the core Biblical commitment to loving others results in societies that care for the weak, the widows, the orphans, lame, blind etc. We are to share one another's burdens. This requires an inclusiveness that seeks to overcome social and racial barriers. Including in the workplace.

Social controls are necessary to check inevitable inequalities in any economic system. While we have freedom to *manage the earth*, so that it grows in fruitfulness, this does not grant freedom to *exploit the earth* till it becomes barren as has occurred in Northern India, or in the destruction of Indonesian forests. This in principle puts a limitation on the production of wealth.

Secondly, production is for the common good, the good of all, not simply the good of the individual. Over-production or mal-distribution or lack of access to necessities are all violations of this principle of service to the common good. Economics must have social goals not simply financial ones. Some have suggested the triple bottom line as a methodology for accomplishing this with corporations, but there is little common agreement.

The Sabbath also indicates that a people-based orientation to efficient production is necessary. Production and wealth-making are to be paced to the needs of our human capacities. This is foundational to the development of community organisations, trade unions, cooperatives, that seek to balance the structuring of the needs of the producers against the needs of those who provide capital (the capitalists).

The Jubilee was a clear modelling of a principle of limits to consumption and speculation. It also indicated the necessity of periodic restitution, for all systems develop inequities and injustices.

The concept of justice is not simply a grand theme but involves diligent scrutiny in every society so that there are just transactions at each point.

The nature of work being good is that products must have intrinsic value. Gambling, for example, is not considered good work for it produces nothing of intrinsic value in a community (apart from its destruction of the lives of many, particularly the poor), thus a good society would not have a gambling casino at the centre of a city.

Due regard to social and ecological consequences of production, the means of production, the relationships within the productive system, the relationships between the earth and its people are thus all inherent in the Biblical narrative and provide a basis for constant critique of all economic systems by Christian prophets.

In the area of New Zealand economics, one could ask, to what extent Evangelicals have enabled society to respect the dignity of the human being. Jane Kelsey, in *Reclaiming the Future: New Zealand and the Global Economy*,[10] documented the effects of overly rapid commitment to the positive benefits of free trade with concomitant loss of jobs in several sectors, including 21,000 in the textiles and clothing sector, the loss of sovereignty over many of our national assets and increase in inequity and insecurity. This is 21,000 people who lost their sense of identity and dignity for a time because of a socialist vision hastily imposed on them. That violates the biblical principles of the worth of personhood.

But one must recognise the right wing American perspectives that often surface in the analysis of economic freedom. Since a very high percentage of New Zealand's GDP is related to exports, we are by necessity committed to a globally open trading structure. However, an *extreme* free trade agenda has demonstrably damaged whole sectors of New Zealand's business; Margaret Thatcher-style selling of New Zealand's assets to foreign investors has sold much of New Zealand's assets that the government managed on behalf of the people to foreigners involved in asset stripping; openness to foreign competition from countries that print billions of dollars is not competition – it can be a tidal wave of dispossession.

Yet one should applaud the attempt to quantify economic freedom which has some roots in the Biblical affirmation of private property. At the same time, we need to reflect from a Biblical perspective whether these measures fulfil the Jubilee mandate of the scriptures to freedom for individual workers not just corporate and financial interests, of periodic redistribution (in post-modern societies this tends to be though yearly redistribution of the tax take through social welfare means).

Alternative approaches might consider the quality of distribution, the protections of workers' rights rather than the freedom from regulation that protects their rights, the sustaining of an underlying health care and educational systems, the right to free tertiary education, the ratio of income of top executives to workers (Switzerland debated a 7:1 ratio), all as elements essential to national economic freedoms.

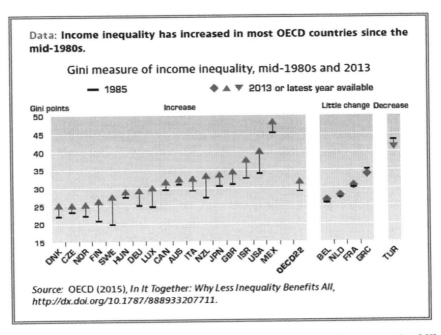

Figure 11: The Gini coefficient is a measure of inequality within a country. Over a generation, NZ has moved from being one of the most egalitarian societies to one that is significantly divided between rich and poor.

1

10. Kingdom and Capitalism

God-Infused Kiwi Capitalism

Our discussion progresses to a biblical critique of macro-economic systems. In this chapter we will consider some Capitalist development theories. Since the axioms of Christian development theology are rooted in revealed truth, and integrated around the person and nature of God, they both clash with all humanistic theories, and at the same time uphold parts of these theories which are consistent with Biblical revelation. Critique, means we are always ambivalent towards any system – affirming and opposing at the same time, as systems reflect both the nature of God in collective human endeavour that is in his image, and the horrific nature of collective human sin built into structures of evil – and everything in-between.

Christians live in an uneasy relationship to culture and in this case to the economic sphere of our culture. We are in the world but not of the world.

Because we are created in God's image, we reflect that image, whether as Christians or non-believers who are still made in his image. And collectively we reflect the social image of God the *usness*, the trinity. He functions in unity, as Jesus describes throughout the book of John. The three in one is a collective and we function collectively made in his image. In the economic realm, over generations, each society makes collective decisions, and these form social and economic structures, and contractual relationships.

Thus our economic structures, and in New Zealand, our socialised capitalist structure is built on centuries of that reflection of God's economic principles, often by godly men and women. At the roots of Capitalism is our national processes to increase *productivity*, and a serious national commitment to *creativity* as evidenced in the expansion of the creative arts education in schools and universities. We have always been a *hard-working* people. And the principle of *rest* has continued in our commitment to the long weekend, despite the recent inroads from the supermarkets, alcohol industry, and secularists to eliminate Sunday rest and Christian public holidays. We have protected our summer beach vacations because, as a people, we know the imperative of rest for emotional survival.

Our socialised Capitalism is also balanced with a *cooperative* collectivism in our public health care system, and the structures of business formation, cooperatives, board governance, contract laws etc., that facilitate people working together and caring for each other. The determined efforts towards racial reconciliation have deeply affirmed the cooperative nature of Maori tribal society as something *Pakeha* wish to engage, and learn from – this is different to other countries and a great honour on the global stage. We see social integration as a serious national goal.

And *redistribution* is integral to our socialised Capitalism, and social welfare system, job retraining, university grants, care for the elderly. All of this built on land and home *ownership,* the foundation of Capitalism. All of these have developed within a framework of *freedom of the individual* to speak, to worship to be to work.

Thus we see our ten principles culturally reflect that nature of God within the Kiwi soul. They are *good* things, just as God said all that he made was *good.* If the following critiques aspects of these, it is not with a view to rejecting our socialised capitalist economy and our history.

Yet, on the other side of our relationship to culture, Christians are prophets against corrupted sinful culture. Our collective sinful nature creates sinful structures – the tendency towards *non-productivity,* the *limiting of creativity* in mindless modernist mechanistic factories, the pressure to create contexts of *overwork* or of those who are *loathe to work* hard, the *expropriation of lands* so that land ownership is not feasible, the *greed* which consumes but does not seek to *redistribute* to the needy - these are all human violations of the ten principles we began with.

Historic Christianity has a long literature about spiritual warfare. We are called to confront the Powers of this age by destroying false philosophies.[2] Those powers may legitimately be exegeted as *"isms"* - Capitalism, Marxism, Socialism, Nationalism, Globalism…[3]

Yet, if one lifts their voice against the dark side of Capitalism, rocks are immediately thrown. I recently put one post on one of the evils of Capitalism on Facebook and got thirty-four enthusiastic responses – only four on the topic, and some of them quite aggressively critical, but totally without understanding! Any criticism is seen as biting the hand that feeds us, like criticizing our grandma! Capitalism is deeply mixed up with political slogans. We need clear discernment, and understanding of the issues, if we are to speak for Biblical justice.

For those friends who are fundamentalists, Pentecostals and evangelicals, there is always a suspicion that in engaging in such issues of justice somehow we have lost our way from a pure gospel commitment. I suggest to folks that it may take some years to grasp the content of the previous chapters; that the gospel is about all of life including economics; it results not just discipling of individuals but of the nations *and* their political economic structures. In the meantime it may be helpful to muse on the prophecy 600 years before Jesus, *Behold, my servant whom I uphold, I will put my Spirit on him…he will not fail till he has established justice in the earth.*[4] True Pentecostals, true evangelicals, people of the Holy Spirit, are justice-makers.

What is Global Capitalism?

So what is the current global Power we are confronted with? Definitions of global Capitalism are a poor beginning for it is a constantly evolving dynamic covering a diverse range of configurations.

R.H. Tawney in his *Religion and the Rise of Capitalism*, identifies the period between 1500 and 1700 where the church lost its engagement with the economic sphere. The mediaeval Europe that was the pre-curser civilisation to modern civilisation can be considered ended at the Treaty of Westphalia in 1648, where European states made a contract to not war over religion - in essence the end of Christendom into countries with diverse religious traditions where the Church no longer was supreme authority. By 1700, the ground for evaluating economic theory and practice was evacuated by Christian moralists and came into the realm of scientific method under the secular States.

Capitalism has always been global. The beginnings of Capitalism go back to the fifteenth Century where life was settled and all knew their place within the feudal context. Growing international trade, improved transport, and increased capital enabled larger corporations, not dissimilar to the explosion of larger organisations today as nations become urbanised and amass capital in urban centres.

Analysis of these new principles was the contribution of the brilliant and extensive Adam Smith's *Wealth of the Nations* (1776) as, in five books, he evaluated the transition from *mercantilism* to a modern capitalist context.

That expansion of capital and creation of an expanded class of capitalists in England came from expansion of global trade (supported by piracy). And the evil of the English enclosures. And beyond that it was a continuity of the system of Lords and serfs. In the enclosures, the Lords of England legally stole the traditional *commons* land of the peasants where they would graze their flocks, by fencing them in. Millions were left without income and migrated to the cities. At the same time the emergence of large mills and beginnings of mechanisation in the cities needed excess labour. Thus the capitalists, at the foundation of Capitalism were no more than robber barons who moved ill-gotten gain from their rural estates to the new urban explosion of England and Europe. The serfs who had produced wealth on the farm, now became the workers producing wealth in the factory. These were supplemented by a massive slave trade providing cheap labour.

Adam Smith's definitions are reflected 120 year later in an old Oxford Economics textbook on my bookshelf (1). An organisation of business (2). upon a large scale (3). by an employer or company of employers (4). possessing an accumulated stock of wealth (5). with which to acquire (a). tools and (b). raw materials and (c). to hire labour, so as (6). to produce an increased quantity of wealth (profit).[5]

Today, Capitalism as a popular term, is a very broad term for multiple expressions of political economic systems that encompass freedoms for:

1. The natural emergence of small businesses at the grassroots of free societies (both the businesses and freedom are things we all applaud).
2. The historic development of multinational large scale businesses.
3. These have evolved through various stages of Capitalism in different countries: post-Mercantilism, Fordism, post-Fordism, Keynesian economics, neoliberalism, global Capitalism...
4. American Capitalism also needs differentiating from more socialised European Capitalisms.
5. Moderated by various socialised approaches within countries, usually at odds with the banking sectors pursuit of profit.

By 2016, global-national Capitalism had morphed into: (1) an economic and political system in which (2) a country's trade and industry (3) are controlled by private owners (though the stock market, or as unlisted companies or cooperatives) (4) who facilitate rapid expansion of new innovations. (5). It is dependent on a wide base of cheap available labour, including migrants and undocumented workers, based on governmental migration approaches though increasing automation mitigates this dependence, and increases dependence on a highly skilled workforce.

(6). It has not existed without governmental intervention and structuring of legal frameworks. (7) The system includes central banks which are privately owned (and ownership is rarely publicly disclosed) that monitor the creation of new money through local banks, as they leverage deposits with loan moneys. (8) The creation of new money is largely regulated through global mechanisms, particularly the International Bank of Settlements in Basel, Switzerland. (9) Global trade is executed within the legal framework of secretly negotiated international treaties minimally subject to democratic processes within the countries signing.

Globalisation

Over the last decades we are facing a far different creature. The globally interlinked descendants of these various phases now connected with the global oligarchy of Fortune 500 companies that compete with nation-states. All these are supported by the International Monetary Fund (IMF), the World Bank, the *Bank for International Settlements* in Switzerland, the stock markets in London, New York and Tokyo, and world trade agreements. All are involved in processes for economic rule and exploitation of the planet.

The Transmogrification of Money

Economics begins with money. Capitalism cannot be understood apart from understanding its linkage to monetary production. Money is a traditional unit storing value, a unit of account. It used to be for much of history, a discrete object such as a piece of copper used as common exchange within a society. More recently it has become symbolic pieces of paper with governmental seals. And yet more recently, it is a series of 1's and 0's in a global network of computers. Whoever controls the production of paper money exercises great powers. Thomas Jefferson, US President in the debate over the Re-charter of the Bank Bill in 1809 spoke:

> *If the American people ever allow private banks to control the issue of their currency, first by inflation, then by deflation, the banks...will deprive the people of all property until their children wake-up homeless on the continent their fathers conquered.... The issuing power should be taken from the banks and restored to the people, to whom it properly belongs. –*

Woodrow Wilson signed the 1913 Federal Reserve Act in the United States. A few years later he wrote:

> *I am a most unhappy man. I have unwittingly ruined my country. A great industrial nation is controlled by its system of credit. Our system of credit is concentrated. The growth of the nation, therefore, and all our activities are in the hands of a few men. We have come to be one of the worst ruled, one of the most completely controlled and dominated Governments in the civilized world no longer a Government by free opinion, no longer a Government by conviction and the vote of the majority, but a Government by the opinion and duress of a small group of dominant men.*

The monetary system has been morphing rapidly over the last hundred years into an international electronic network which is now 20-50 times larger than the real economies. Thus, during the Brexit news the commentators stated, "the world just lost 3 trillion dollars". This was not real money but created computer-defined money.

- It is a largely unregulated global network (As we have seen earlier, greed requires regulation).

- It has become volatile, as larger and larger flows occur in more and more compressed time frames.

The network includes:

- the world's trading markets in things like oil, milk, timber, steel...
- stocks (direct investment in capital of companies)
- bonds (ownership of the debt of companies), futures (betting against the future fluctuations of these) – these have little international regulation
- currency – globally related to the floating dollar, which used to be related to gold but is now related to no fixed real world entity.

Divorced from a direct connection to a physical reality of gold or silver, currency has also become a speculative instrument. Changes in demand and supply between countries affect the values of currencies, but increasingly speculators can control those values. This speculation in the money economy has hurt investment in the real economy. For example, New Zealand companies can no longer effectively set export and import prices in advance, as exchange rates and interest rates oscillate dramatically, dependent on the gambling of investors.

The 2008-9 crisis resulted because of this fundamental change in economics. Supply and demand now have little to do with price changes of real items; time frames have become compressed; and a dual economy has emerged. This dual economy consists of:

- *the real economy*: real products, real trade, research and services, factory workers , doctors, building roads... This has become impoverished as money has been drawn into:
- *the financial economy* which is 20 to 50 times larger. It is essentially contracts built on paper money, which in turn is built on the real economy.

This latter has a valid basis for assisting companies to capitalize and manage their assets. Many middle class folks have retirement savings invested. However, the value of real production is multiplied to such an extent with many different forms of contract, that a major contraction could destroy all before it.

Private Ownership as the Foundation of Capitalism

The *right to own* is a prerequisite to freedom, and to building capital. But Galbraith indicates that housing will never be fully provided for the poor in a Capitalist system. Thus most Capitalist countries have some form of socialised redistribution that helps poor people access ownership of housing.

To the extent that people own their own homes is the extent they can capitalise the formation of small businesses. New Zealand's housing program in the mid-1900's provided access for all to reasonable housing, and was the envy of the world. The sale of these assets in the 1990's has led to a very different context today.

As seen in earlier chapters, the scriptures affirm private ownership. But in the scriptures, ownership is tempered by social responsibility. The implication is that non-profit or governmental involvement in housing is essential.[6] While housing and land is the foundation of wealth savings and hence capital formation within Capitalism, Capitalism will not by itself provide sufficient housing for the poor.

Production Basis of Wealth vs Phony Paper Money

The real productivity of the world faces some limited resources. Investment of capital is an essential element in expanding productivity. However, the continual expansion of paper money based on paper agreements, bonds, stocks, and contracts faces the uncertainties of unreality and is anchored in stock exchanges based on a form of logical yet poorly supervised gambling.

A Biblical critique begins in the fundamental principal of production in the Kingdom for the purposes of both provision and giving (II Corinthians 8: 2,15). The world's system is one of getting. Biblical Economics starts in the cross as it cuts our basic instinct to acquire. Out of the giving, comes mustard seed production. Giving (investing) capital to provide resources for expansion of production to meet needs can be an act of love that provides both new resources and work for people. Extracting money from such production for non-productive speculation is the opposite of love. It is a hatred.

A grassroots network fighting the escalating production of paper money in Britain, *Positive Money*,[7] engages in significant discussion on finding alternatives to the present process, such that money does not flow to the banks but to the people.[8] One of their understandings is that every time a bank writes a mortgage it is creating money. Referring to the European situation, since Quantitative Easing (the creation of paper money by central banks (technically by the local banks giving mortgages) after the 2009 crisis) started, 720 billion euros have been created. This money has flooded financial markets, pushing up house prices and is driving inequality. *QE for People* argues there is an alternative. Central banks could use newly created money to meet the needs of society - to finance infrastructure projects, build affordable housing or by giving it directly to Eurozone citizens.

The above is immensely complicated. But confusing even more because many equate Capitalism with Christianity. In the following sections we will examine the relationship of Capitalism and Christianity, followed by critiques of Capitalism from alternative development theories.

Capitalism and Christianity

Capitalism is not essential for the survival of Christianity. Capitalism also has no special claim on Christian virtue, though Christian values are essential to it success. Both Marxism and Capitalism have equally materialistic views - and goals. Yet Capitalism thrives on the freedom also inherent in Christianity and, as such, is more compatible with a free society built on Christian values.[9]

The collapse of the Iron Curtain was a symbol that Capitalism has proven far better for the poor than Communism, so is a preferred choice between the two. Production of wealth precedes distribution of wealth, and Capitalism enables better *production*.

Thus there has been an uneasy symbiosis between Capitalism and Christianity. Yet many Christian thinkers consistently talk of a third way between Capitalism and Marxism.

Dependence of Capitalism on Morality

A healthy capitalist economy is dependent on moral standards:

> *Without the civilizing force of universal moral standards, particularly honesty, trust, self-respect, integrity and loyalty, the marketplace quickly degenerates* (Brookes, 1986).

Max Weber, the great voice at the founding of sociology, in his thesis on *The Protestant Work Ethic and the Birth of Capitalism* (Weber, 2010), analysed the effects of the various great religious traditions on economic values and structures, demonstrating how the reformation and the Puritans gave specific legitimacy to private property, profit and wealth creation as a *calling*. He predicted the rise of the *Chinese dragons* (Singapore, Taiwan, Hong Kong, South Korea), indicating values from Confucianism that would more likely contribute to effective wealth creation and Capitalism. Diligence and thrift derived from perspectives on holiness, were seen as part of godly character – qualities critical to production of wealth.

Gunnar Myrdal, in his 10 year study that identified twenty-nine causes of national poverty in Asia, *Asian Drama*, analyses the negative effects of fatalism in Hinduism, Buddhism and animism – the belief that one has no control over one's destiny often because of fear of the control by spirits - on entrepreneurial activity.

123

Brian Griffiths, Christian economic advisor to Margaret Thatcher (1985) discusses the coincidence of the breakdown of British and Western society values since the 1950's at the same time as what he describes as continuous economic crises in the West. He suggests that the progression from the Puritanism of Weber to the secular humanist culture of the 1980's has resulted in the loss of these core values. I would suggest that the breakdown of Kiwi culture into postmodernism has produced further loss of values. Some contrasts are suggested (not researched but suggested) in Fig 12, for discussion, extending my work in *The Spirit of Christ and the Postmodern City*.

The crisis of 2009 in the United States reflects this shift in values, involving financial men in grey suits earning ludicrous bonuses for deals in paper money that bear little resemblance to the realities of production, and eventually establishing products so removed from production that they nearly crashed the financial systems.

Backed onto large bonuses for short-term gains, Lehman Brothers had leveraged its actual assets to thirty times their value. That meant only a 3% shift in markets made them illiquid. This was not only greed, but reflects a lack of prudence. Its bankruptcy caused the near-collapse of 2009.

In the *Global Economic Forum* report of 2009, New Zealand was ranked second in terms of corporate ethics. That is a worthy statement and one that needs to be held on to carefully, particularly as for *Pakeha*, the decline of truth and moral values as families collapse does not bode well for future business ethics, and successive governments have increased migration from nations where there is little culture of integrity (though much else culturally worthy of honour), without any training for in-coming migrants in our historic Christian values of truth in business dealings.

Theoretical Debates about Capitalist Development

The Linear Take-Off Theory

William Rostow's theory *The Stages of Economic Growth* (1991) and those that have followed - leading to the *Global Millennial Goals* (Sachs, 2006) to abolish poverty, and to the current World Economic Forum's four stages of growth (2015) - have tried to distil from the experience of rich countries a set of rules which poor countries should follow if they are to take off into self-sustained growth. He described this is a stage taking 20-30 years when the economy and the society of which it is part transform themselves in such a way that economic growth is more or less automatic.

Value	Evangelical England of the 1880's	Secular Humanist 80's in New Zealand	Postmodern Auckland in 21st Century
Centre	Faith and God	Individualism	Hedonism and Mammon
Work	Seen as a calling	As a means to get money	As an accessory to the good life
View of Future	God has a purpose to history and future	Live for today's pleasures	Live for today, for wealth will continue to expand
Savings	Save to provide for future, invest to maximise	Avoid debt, depend on government for future	Live on credit cards and maximise consumption
Budget	Strict balanced budgeting	Casual budgeting,	Live on credit card, Balanced government budget through asset sales
Engine of Economy	Family	Government as engine of redistribution	Global Economy
Locus of Government	Small government	Large nanny state	International Economic Order
Property	Private Property, Privately owned businesses	Increasing State ownership, private property protected	Increasing corporate ownership, but private property protected
Defense of Workers	Trade Unions defending against injustices	Unions raising real incomes; governments break unions	Variable contract laws; decreased defence of workers; mobile workforce
Money	Linked to real production	Linked to currencies controlled by national banks	A means of speculation, 20-50 times the value of real production
Corporate ethics	Evangelical engagement in legislation for corporate management to care for its workforce and ethics of its products	Significant care for workers, partly because of trade union successes over decades, partly mainline church influences Post-Christian culture of integrity largely continues.	Global corporations maximizing profits with an amoral basis in ethical decision-making. Loss of integrity in Pakeha culture. Extensive in-migration from cultures with less integrity. vs. ethical business models

Figure 12: Postmodern values that impact economics.

The preconditions for take-off he determined as being:

- An increase in investment flow in one or more substantial manufacturing sectors (known as leading sectors).
- This leading sector is then the vehicle for the diffusion of new production techniques to other groups and society as a whole needs to respond to these indicators.
- This must go hand in hand with the existence or quick emergence of a responsive political and institutional framework.
- To perpetuate this growth a high percentage of real income needs to be returned to productive investments.
- The availability of a cheap source of labour is essential. Today we might add, skilled, educated and creative labour coupled with automation.

With this very brief overview let us make a few critiques from the scriptures and development theories. I will not present all critiques of such a theory but just those pertinent to Christian theology.

Dualism

The first major criticism is of the concept of encouraging *dualism* in a society, a theory popularised in *Economics and Economic Policy of Dual Societies.*[10] This dualism is where a portion of the population enjoy the fruits of modern society while the masses remain locked in abject poverty- the rich get richer and the poor get poorer.

The biblical comment on this stems from the concept of *shalom* which has meanings of,

> *well-being, of freedom, from what threatens this well-being and fulfilment, of freedom from want, and injustice, freedom from external warfare and from division within. It is a common participation in and harmony of the people with its leaders.*[11]

All development programs involve improving the lot of a few for the good of the whole and hence involve inequalities,[12] but to deliberately create a disparity, or to fail to provide significant development plans for the bottom 40% is to destroy shalom deliberately and must be prophetically denounced.

Dualism tears the shalom of developing countries in pieces, creates greater and greater poverty for the rural poor and urban workers, and greater wealth for an elite class. Not only so, it destroys the cultural fabric of the society, another essential stabilizing factor in shalom. By causing the rich agricultural barons to invest their money in the industrial leading sector, little is reinvested in the rural areas, hence no intermediate rural industry is developed, to create employment in the rural areas. The result is massive urbanisation and millions of squatters and slum dwellers in megacities. Fortunately New Zealand for many decades reinvested into agricultural areas.[13] More recently that focus has decreased.

Throughout the scriptures, God continually sought to equalise the discrepancy between rich and poor. This oppression of the poor by the rich is also perpetuated in the continued suppression of workers' wages in the expectation that eventually the greater majority will benefit. Perhaps the ringing words of James are pertinent here:

> *Come now you rich, weep and howl for the miseries that are coming on you...behold the wages of the labourers who moved your fields which kept you back by fraud, cry out; and the cries of the harvesters have reached the Lord of hosts. You have lived on earth in luxury and in pleasure; you have fattened your hearts in a day of slaughter. You have condemned, you have killed the righteous; they do not resist you.[14]*

This Biblical concept of unity within cities is current within urban planning thought. UN Habitat address the need for *harmonious cities* where barriers of race, class, economics are broken down.[15]

Dependency

A further consequence of the application of Rostow's theories is described in a number of theories classified under the title of *dependency theories*. Andre Gunder Frank identified how the economy of the third world country becomes a satellite of the colonial powers and that of the rural areas of the megacities that control their empires. The flow of money and natural resources is to the megacity, which exploit countries by a number of means, primary amongst which is their multinationals. Immanuel Wallerstein extended Frank's theories into *World System Theories*.

In this sense, New Zealand is a classically dependent country, although massive efforts to diversify after Britain cut the umbilical cord to our dairy products have kept us from falling completely out of the OECD (Organization for Economic Cooperation and Development, a linkage of the world's richest democracies). Nevertheless, we export largely raw and cheap agricultural products in exchange for importing expensive industrial products. And as 15 of the 17 banks in our banking system (be it Westpac or National Bank or ANZ or ...) are largely owned by Australia or the UK, all of these transactions pay a "tax" on any profits that ends up in the owner's hands overseas, thus structurally locking us into dependency, just as most former British colonies are locked in.

Written in the midst of the unceasing changes of international alliances in the Middle East, the scriptures are not silent on such dependencies. Leviticus gives a vignette analysis of the effects of righteousness on an economy contrasted with the effects of corruption and unrighteousness. Amongst the effects it talks of are *you shall sow your crops in vain, for your enemies will eat them.*[16]

It is not God's desire that rich business men and women, politicians and businessmen should sell their own birthright to foreign nations. Hence, Christians in positions where they can influence such policies must seek to change them. God's desire for Israel was that they become a nation, that they be slaves no longer. God has broken their chains and would make them walk with dignity.[17]

National freedom is inherent in the gospel. In my first classes in development studies in Manila in 1980, it became apparent that the selling of assets, land, banks and businesses to foreign corporations was a serious step towards becoming a dependent nation. This was done in the name of "foreign investment". The latter is needed if productivity is to increase, but the principle of social responsibility necessitates that the profits of such investment largely remain within a country and are not sucked offshore.

However, those national leading businessmen, economists and politicians who can make some gain from such sales have counter-arguments. In a well-researched report on *New Zealand Global Links,*[18] the Executive Director of the New Zealand Initiative (that does research to assist businesses to invest in New Zealand) states that:

> *Economists typically support not just the free movement of goods and services but also the flow of capital between jurisdictions…The economics behind this general support for free trade and free capital flows are well researched and established - and have been for centuries.*

That leaves no room for argument does it!! Strange, that in development economics in almost any third world country or among New Zealand development workers, that opinion is soundly rejected!! Free trade for smaller nations leads to both dependency and exploitation of resources. Fair trade is what is desired. And this accords with the Biblical notion of *a just balance.*

Asset sales are a complex issue (who would wish to have the task of minister in charge of asset sales?) as shown in a treasury document that identifies many options in a number of case studies.[19] New Zealand was forced by the Muldoon era excesses into a downsizing of government. There is a lot of merit in the government exiting from managing businesses that would be better managed by businessmen, and have no social or strategic value for New Zealanders. There are other assets which belong to the people. The government has a mandate to manage, but it does not necessarily have a mandate to dispose of those.

The Government has sought to put conditions on sales (difficult to enforce), and has consistently preferred selling assets to New Zealand investors. But our internal resources are limited. The referendum in 2013, quite clearly confirmed that after $23,790,670,000,000 of asset sales (New Zealand Treasury, 2014), 66% of New Zealanders are opposed to selling essential assets to overseas investors. The current prime minister ignored the referendum.

On the flip side, New Zealand has strived to negate the worst aspects of asset sales. New Zealand's score on the OECD's FDI *Regulatory Restrictiveness Index*, which measures the extent to which a country's regulations limit against Foreign Investment, remains far above both the non-OECD and OECD averages, being placed as the seventh most astute OECD member in protecting national ownership. UNCTAD's *Attraction Index* ranks New Zealand, 146 of 186 countries, meaning the wealthy find it easier to buy resources elsewhere.

Jim Anderton's formation of *Kiwibank* was one step in reversing this kind of dependency by New Zealand banks. But the international pressure on politicians to sell publicly-owned enterprise into the hands of foreign capitalists is intense (even though these had been capitalised by the people of New Zealand over decades). Yet as Mike Moore, one of the clique involved in the early sales, reflects in his autobiography, what option was there, when former Prime Minister, Rob Muldoon, had left us paying 19c on the dollar in interest. From his perspective, with the money from asset sales, New Zealand was able to expand its education and health systems. We all face such dilemmas at times as cash flow problems require conversion of assets into cash.

> **A Just Balance**
>
> Free trade for smaller nations leads to both dependency and exploitation of resources. Fair trade is what is desired. And this accords with the Biblical notion of *a just balance*. Investment is needed but this is different to asset stripping.

Selling the crown jewels had devastating effects on our rail system, allowed for massive destruction of native forests as European pine is planted to replace them for the sake of profit, destroyed the integration and efficiency of one of the world's best electricity systems in the name of *competition* i.e. letting foreign companies gain control and hence follow profit-based outcomes without consideration of social objectives. This latter was a wider global push by US electricity companies (who had no apparent idea of the importance and benefit of a unified state-owned electrical system in a small country) to gain control of electricity systems in other countries. Our rail system had to be bought back at great loss after being fleeced by an American company. The concept of essential national assets that cannot be sold has become part of the NZ psyche (though not of the National party leadership, it seems).

On the side of justifying such sales, forestry for example, has moved from a loss generating government department to a highly profitable industry, with investments flowing back into value added processing operations, not just exportation of logging. I say that, tongue in cheek, as necessary investments range from 4-6 billion in estimate. Actual investments are a pittance compared with this figure.[20]

Bill English has also attempted to spuriously document the usefulness of the banks being owned by foreign companies, in that each time they create a loan they add money to the NZ money supply. This is one process, as far as I can tell, that is pushing up the global price of urban land, but others might be able to explain the rationale for such a statement.[21]

Bryce Wilkinson in *New Zealand's Global Links: Foreign Ownership and the Status of New Zealand's Net International Investment,*, a quality research document, funded by those with aims to increase investment in New Zealand, shows that:

- Despite popular myth, New Zealanders actually earn more than they spend. National resident unit savings has been positive for the last 38 of the last 41 years.
- Despite concerns to the contrary, Asians are not taking over New Zealand. In fact, in 2012 Australians owned 55% of foreign investment in New Zealand, while ASEAN nations owned only 3.1%.
- If New Zealanders are to become tenants in their own country, it is more likely the landlord will be the government, not foreign investors. Of the 28.7 million hectares in New Zealand, the report estimates that 1 million are owned by foreigners, and the Department of Conservation alone manages 8.5 million.
- Offshore investment is a two-way street. New Zealand is not a 'takeover' target by foreign investors. In fact, the OECD regards New Zealand's regime for screening inwards investment as one of the most restrictive in the world.
- New Zealand has been heavily dependent on international capital since colonial days, and this is normal for a young, growing country.

In a related issue, the ability of Chinese to now shift money to overseas properties is pushing up property prices globally, not just in New Zealand.

33% of housing sales in Vancouver are by Chinese investors for example.[22] A search on the web shows the same set of comments from cities around the Pacific, "House prices keep escalating. Increasing numbers of Chinese buying." That is not a racist statement. One understands the genuine desire by wealthy Chinese who have worked hard and saved hard to invest their capital in safer contexts, as they face uncertainties in China until it regularizes some of its legal systems.

To escape such an environment, investors have to circumvent the Chinese laws that forbid taking more than $50,000 out of China by recruiting relatives and others to carry the money out. They then have to circumvent the NZ investor laws that are aimed at investment in industry. Indeed, globally, most migrants face having to find some loophole in laws to migrate, so such aberrations do not then mean these are criminals. In the corruption of Brazil and China and elsewhere, survival often requires finding a way through a loophole between corruption and conflicting laws. So surely in New Zealand the same is true, right? In our personal caring for many migrants in our home we have a humanitarian involvement, but most of our friends face multiple failed attempts to get around migration law and end up returning home.

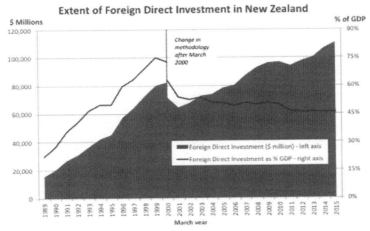

Figure 13: Foreign investment as a % of GNP.

Source: International Investment Position, National Accounts - Statistics New Zealand

But apart from these very understandable legal violations in attempts to find economic freedom in a just nation, we have a problem - young New Zealanders or Canadians can no longer afford to buy their first house. Their birthright is gone. Protection against free capital flows into housing *by non-*

residents is essential in such a context, not free trade. Again this goes back to a principle of solidarity, of social responsibility. If migrants come committed to becoming part of society, all affirm their attempts. But if simply New Zealand is seen as a place to make money and whisk away its profits, then the society should reject such people or multinationals. Fortunately, the banks are taking action even as the government has failed to do so.[23]. That phrase "non-resident" is crucial, when one attends auctions for Auckland houses and discovers a room full of people visiting for a few days to buy at double the real market price, and then return to China. When people genuinely migrate and invest their lives in building a nation, it is a very different story, and such are welcomed by New Zealand's immigration policies.

Affirmation of the British Jack on our flag is not an affirmation of dependency, but of our security in independence from Britain, yet desire to maintain cultural roots. But in the last decades, we have become an increasingly dependent nation, losing control of banks, land, and ownership of productive capacity. The amount of money leaving New Zealand to foreign investors is about the same as our milk powder and seafood industry incomes.

Biblical Critiques of Capitalism

Having affirmed grassroots New Zealand Capitalism, we need to examine alternative Biblical perspectives, that provide critical critiques of many aspects of globalisation.[24] These are perspectives generally held in the development studies community whose mandate is to comprehend how to liberate oppressed peoples.

Humans are of Infinite Worth

At this point, we need to return to our principle one, *the value of humanity* in the scriptures. Human beings were made in the image of God, and because of this are of intrinsic worth, and infinite value – each man and woman. This is brilliantly described in Prov 4:31, *He who oppresses a poor person insults his maker.* Even to give a cup of water is upholding that reflected image of God in humanity.[25]

God is a creator, so also human beings are creative. Our work too reflects God's character for God works. We require rest to maintain our creative strength. Humans are not machines.

Both Marxism and forms of Capitalism differ from the Biblical view in their concept of humanity. Both seek to accomplish the good of society as a whole at the cost of the individual. It matters little whether the individual is crushed as a cog in the machinery of production (Capitalism) or as a cog in the worship of the Government (Marxism). In both cases humanity is at the service of the economy.[26] Economics is God! The economics of the Government is God!

In contrast, Christians understand that humanity, like God (a trinity) is also a fellowshipping, communicating, communal creature. Over creation, humanity is ruler, but with another human we are not rulers but brothers and sisters. Jesus told us call no person *master* or *father* for you are *all brothers* and you have one teacher, one Lord, one father. *He who is greatest among you shall be your servant.*[27]

By placing the leader as servant, underneath others, he precludes any possibility of using position to use, abuse, or oppress others, not that he abolishes social roles rather he equalises men and women in these roles.

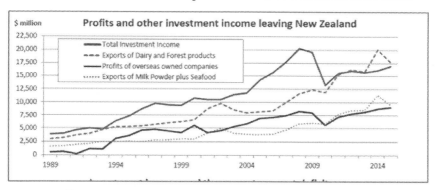

Figure 14: Profits and their investment income leaving New Zealand.

Hence we dare not uplift one part of society at the cost of another. This destroys not only human dignity, but also fellowship and community between these parts of the culture.

Capitalism, Greed and Contentment

Capitalism errs in that an excessive amassing of wealth is its prime motive and competition its supreme law. Ezekiel comments on this:

Behold this was the sin of your sister Sodom; she and her daughters had pride, surfeit of food and prosperous ease but did not aid the poor and needy.[28]

Elsewhere we are told that *the love of money is the root of all evil,*[29] and that *covetousness is as the sin of idolatory.*[30] Jesus tells us that if we have food and clothing we should be content.[31]

On the other hand, the scriptures give many principles for successful business, especially in Proverbs. There is no criticism of making reasonable profit that is based on fairness and generosity in business dealings.[32]

Humanity as Slave of Economics

Capitalism turns everything - art, music, literature, even beauty itself, into commodities to be bought and sold. It turns human beings into commodities. Not just the factory workers - the physicians, the artists, the poets, the musicians.

They all must sell themselves in order to survive. This perhaps can be stated of all capitalist, socialist or feudal economies in the modern period. Jaques Ellul, the French theologian-philosopher in his *Technological Society*, predicted the rise of the technological society and its definition of our humanness – in many ways this is regardless of the political economic system.

As Christians, we must resist the creation of commodity man, be constantly on guard as the government seeks to turn education into a commodity, senior health care into a commodity, creativity itself into a commodity, the beach *bach* into a commodity. And ourselves. Our forefathers fought for 40 hour weeks, but the destruction of the power of the trade unions mean that most of us now work fifty to sixty hours to survive and many in two jobs. Sunday was sacred, but how can you commoditise that one day outside the system – so by stealth, business interests have extended Sunday trading. Tertiary education was a right for Kiwis, now it is a commodity for capitalist-owned banks.

> ### Commodification
>
> Capitalism turns everything - art, music, literature, even beauty itself, into commodities to be bought and sold. It turns human beings into commodities. Not just the factory workers - the physicians, the artists,

We must fight for conditions where children of God, and all are his children, can live to be creative, live in security, with secure incomes, with time to rest, time to be as families, just as our forefathers struggled.

This chapter has critiqued some of the evils of Capitalism. These have been modified by the consistent fight of those who have been committed to Biblical principles of equality, ownership, justice, cooperation Not that all who have fought for these would name Christian values as their motivation) over the last centuries into what is now our mixed Capitalist system. In the next chapter we examine other godly dynamics within Capitalism that enable it to create work, wealth and liberty for billions.

11. Creativity, Innovation and Entrepreneurship

Technological Innovation

Capitalism is built on the creativity of those at the grassroots of society. It is frequently commented, though debateable, that small business is its primary driver. Others would point to the multinationals. Without the capital of multinationals, many creative inventions would not now be developed. An intel chip for example need to generate $3 billion over its first two years to be economically viable. It takes five years to make. A human brain has 100 billion neurons. By 2026, our computers will have more transistors in their chips. This is a remarkable testimony to the effectiveness of Capitalism in the harnessing of creativity for the welfare of billions of mankind.[1]

In the pastoral context of the Old Testament we have examined *land* and *resources*. But we live in what is now called the fourth industrial revolution where the technological speed of ideas is multiplying exponentially. Jacques Ellul, the great French philosopher, sociologist and theologian wrote of this in the 1980's in the *Technological Society*, predicting the increasingly technologically-determined man. We need to take the principles from these Biblical contexts and apply them to current *industrial technologies* and from this decade on to *information technologies*.

Creativity, which underlies innovation is a critical element for survival in such an environment. Innovation combines *creativity* (2) and *management* (8) skills. It is inherent in godliness as it marks the very core nature of God the creator, and Jesus the liberator, who brings the *freedom* (10). A nation that is full of creativity and innovation is perhaps not too far from God![2]

> *We are a nation of enthusiastic adopters. We embrace technological change and its associated benefits…the pace at which technology is transforming our lives is exponential.*[3]

This is critical for survival.

> *Disruptive technologies, which create new markets and displace existing ones, are the new normal, and given New Zealand's relatively healthy economy and flexible regulatory environment, we appear to be well placed to evolve and prosper.*[4]

New Zealand banking systems, for example, are ranked as number one globally in pioneering new payment methodologies.[5] Technology companies are also experiencing high revenue growth and success in the United States markets. A new approach to funding, peer to peer lending such as Harmoney, or TradeMe, grew to US$267 million in New Zealand.

Psychological Theories - Entrepreneurship

An early approach to development economics was a search for those sociological and psychological factors critical to the emergence of a significant class of entrepreneurs. The fundamental thesis, was that internal value systems are the critical factors in transforming the environmental factors. McLelland defined these values, within multiple studies and a global search for *n-achievement*.[6]

He extended the work of sociologist, Max Weber[7] who analysed religious impact on economic organization of the society. He identified religious beliefs as a driving or restraining force for generating entrepreneurial activity. Religious beliefs play a crucial role in determining the behaviour or actions of the entrepreneur towards generating or limiting profit. Weber was the first among the social scientists, to posit that entrepreneurial growth is dependent upon ethical values.

This was in opposition to other theories of development (mostly stemming from sociological and economic world views) that stress the systems as the critical factors in national development. As Marx says:

> *The mode of production in material life determines the general character of the social, political and spiritual processes of life. It is not the consciousness of men and women that determine their existence, but on the contrary their social existence that determine their consciousness.*[8]

(Hence his rejection of God as a tool of the bourgeoisie).

The Bible affirms the internal value systems as causative of national prosperity, though not neglecting systems, structural changes and institutionalisation of values. Jesus moved from legal structures that bound his nation to values systems as preeminent. *It is from within, from the heart of a person that come lust, theft, murder, adultery covetousness, wickedness, deceit...*[9] The whole focus of Jesus is captured in the beatitudes of the Sermon on the Mount – about meekness, purity, peacemaking, the hunger for righteousness – values! The Kingdom which he brought is a Kingdom *not of food and drink, but of joy and peace in the Holy Spirit.*[10] Christian growth occurs as we are *not conformed to this world, but transformed by the renewal of our minds.*[11] These all indicate that Jesus and followers were focussed on a transformation of values in the progression towards bringing justice on earth - Jesus mandate from the servant psalms of Isaiah.

Two aspects of these psychological theories are significant for Christians:

> *Studies of the family have shown, for instance, that for a boy three factors are important in producing high "n" achievement (a measure of achievement*

orientation), parents' high standards of achievement, warmth and encouragement, and a father who is not dominating and authoritarian… Other studies have shown that fathers must be respected by their sons; but after the boy is capable of achieving something for himself, his father must stop directing every step he takes if the boy is to develop a strong concern for achievement. [12]

Another study shows that *the two great waves of achievement concern in England were each associated with Protestant reform or revival.* For example, *The strong concern for Christian perfection in this world tended to produce an achievement orientation in Methodist parents and their sons, which turned boys to business.*[13] Fifty years after the revivals the country reached a peak of achievement as these men and women entered national leadership. As the Bible says, *Righteousness exalts a nation.*[14]

Woodberry,[15] in a more recent, ground-breaking, statistically analysed study expands on McLelland and Max Weber by studying the effects of Protestant missions globally on social transformation:

> *This article demonstrates historically and statistically that conversionary Protestants (CPs) influenced both the distribution of resources in societies and the rise and spread of stable democracy around the world.*
>
> *CPs influenced democracy directly by shaping democratic theory and institutions and indirectly by creating religious incentives for elites to disperse economic and political power. CPs wanted people to read the Bible, thus they initiated mass education and mass printing. Moreover, organizational forms and tactics that CPs developed to spread their faith proved useful for sustaining long-term, nonviolent social movements. CPs used these new organizational forms and tactics to transform their home societies and to moderate colonialism. When faced with CP competition, other groups copied these innovations. Without CP competition, they did not and these innovations were delayed for decades, even centuries. Thus, CP competition drastically increased ordinary people's access to education, printed material, news, and organizational resources – whether or not they converted to Protestantism. Moreover, the reform movements spurred by CPs increased the rule of law and fostered the creation of early political parties. Together these factors increased the probability of stable democratic transitions.*

Hagen also tells us of a necessary change in worldview from traditional to modern society. In modern society, an achiever is one who *sees the world as an orderly place* (77). He is one who is in control of his destiny. This is not possible in animistic societies, subject to the whims of spirits, with a cyclical view of life. It is a return to the Biblical concept, that humanity was made to rule and to have dominion over the earth that Hagen *discovered* here.

Both these family changes and the change in the worldview may be generated when significant minority segments of the society follow the scriptures.

Toynbee, in his *Study of History*,[16] developed the thesis that a suppressed minority is the key to changes within civilisations.

In New Zealand, it is evident that the re-emergence of Maori culture, in an environment where treaty reconciliation created opportunities, has released a wave of energy from an oppressed minority. Similarly, in-migration of gifted people from foreign nations such as India, even though the initial years are hard (or perhaps because they are hard), results in enormous energy being expended in their new homeland. Migrants with character and skill are an asset economically to any nation. The demotion from being top level professionals, bankers, businessmen in their home country to being struggling migrants creates a passion to achieve.

These ideas have become the basis for the emergence of both a literature on entrepreneurship, and have jumped disciplines into spiritual formation and organizational psychology in a literature on values. Benjamin Tonna, a Catholic bishop in Malta, and Brian Hall, an Anglican psychotherapist developed a whole progressive system of 125 values in the Hall-Tonna values system.[17]

These build on the classical Greek question as to what is a virtuous person? Aristotle developed a short list including *prudence, temperance, fortitude, and justice*. Aquinas added Paul's list of *faith, hope and charity* to become the seven Christian virtues. From the 1960's a values clarification movement developed, differentiating values form virtues. The human development theories of Kohlberg[18] on moral development in education, Maslow[19] on psychological development stages, and Fowler[20] on *Stages of Faith* contributed to attempts to identify the various life stages and the emergence or prioritising of different values at each stage. They related these to organizational development processes and phases of lifestyle growth.

This values approach has its critics. The major error in these theories is the resultant attempts by developing nations to exorcise those values which are thought to impede economic development and adopt not only Western customs and structures but to internalise Western values. The apparent significant controls by Americans on publishing and definitions used in the global development world, subtly reinforces through a cultural imperialism, these goals to emulate American values. As the philosopher Foucault[21] says, "Knowledge is power" and the significant centralization of knowledge in the marketing of US educational systems globally is a model case study of how that works. We have an alternative collegial global system of eight institutions with the MATUL, but there are few models like it.

Values must be evaluated, not against Western values, but against a universal, infinite reference point – the character of a loving, righteous, unchanging

God. For example in Filipino culture, *hiya* (shame), *pakikisama* (getting on well with people), *utang na loob* (fulfilling mutual obligations) must not be rejected but those aspects of them that are parallel to the values of the beatitudes need to be emphasised and Filipino Christian character developed. One of my students, Sajira Awang, interviewed Filipino Christian leaders. As she compared their values against the literature which put down Filipino cultural leadership from a Western perspective, highlighting negative effects of certain values, she discovered that these leaders among the poor were opposite, displaying the positive side of these values, in genuinely Filipino leadership. Thus Kiwis need to define their own criteria for development. I would suggest that process combines these values of the Kingdom of God with certain Kiwi values.

Relationship Between Righteousness and Achievement

A dollar is not value, but representative of values, and at last of moral values

Ralph Waldo Emerson.

The above theories when linked to economic achievement and entrepreneurship serve the Economic God. Entrepreneurship thus involves an important set of character values. Knowing the God of the scriptures is critical. Not knowing him, means the values become distorted. This emphasis on achievement when secularized can also neglect one very significant factor.

The whole of the Old Testament is a panorama of examples of a principle that Marx, Rostow and others seem perhaps not to have grasped, despite its well-documented historical case studies. We can restate a perspective from Leviticus 26:

> HARD WORK + GOD'S BLESSING = PROSPERITY
>
> HARD WORK – GOD'S BLESSING = ECONOMIC DISASTER

God's blessing is intimately connected to righteousness. We can rewrite the equation (though it is not an equation but a relationship of a nation with an infinite being).

> WORK + RIGHTEOUSNESS = PROSPERITY
>
> WORK – RIGHTEOUSNESS = ECONOMIC DISASTER

The land is fruitful. Humanity is to work to obtain its fruits, but we do not do so in an objective, impersonal universe. It is ordered for God is ordered.

It follows well-defined and observable laws for He is righteous. But it is personal for its creator is personal. His personal involvement can multiply our work a hundredfold, as he blessed Abraham and Jacob and Isaac.

Cooperative Entrepreneurship in the West

I have spent my life training *social entrepreneurs*. The social entrepreneur adds to economic value systems, moral ideals and hence other moral values. From multiplying many organizations through the years, we have put together training for slum leaders at Masters level. We began to realise that several of our courses paralleled what they do in business schools, only we start with people with access to a few hundred or few thousand dollars not millions or hundreds of thousands. The principles are the same, the processes and structures and outcomes different.

There are plenty of courses out there on entrepreneurship, so I won't go into the processes. What we are interested in, in this study, is Biblical reflection on such processes and how these might modify the New Zealand context. The Biblical basis is a powerful motivator and theoretical framework.

> *I was in Mumbai and spoke to a gathering of 200 Christian businessmen on the open air roof of a building. I have rarely had so much fun. In the next 30 minutes I would introduce them to 50 characteristics of the nature of God in Genesis chapter 1 that would transform the business culture of Mumbai. They did not believe it. So we began to unpack these – creativity, productivity, the artistry of God as he made all things good, his ability to create things that create other things… (we can't even get computers to reproduce yet)…*

Small Cooperative Entrepreneurial Businesses

Once poor people have access to capital through ownership of land as collateral or through one of the cooperative savings mechanisms, the capacity to then make money off the capital becomes the next issue to resolve. One of my friends with some years in training of entrepreneurs advised me that 1 in 40 have the gifts, character and skills set (labelled PEC's or Personal Entrepreneurial Characteristics), to be successful in pioneering new businesses.[22]

In classes on urban spirituality, we often begin with a presentation on entrepreneurial spirituality. Faith, wisdom, work, are all essential elements of the spiritual man or woman. They are also integral to Pentecostal teaching. It is also an interesting exercise to contrast the PEC's above with the character of disciples. That character is often forged in young children in contexts of noisy, emotional poor peoples' churches where a vision of vocation is taught, where a sense of destiny is clear, where a constant spirit of faith is encouraged,

'Slumdogs' and Street Boys become Bakers[23]

Abishek Gier is living proof that the gospel of the Kingdom is *good news to the poor*) He is a creative businessman using his gifts to put people in the slums of Delhi to work and to touch their lives in every way. Abishek Gier had such a desire to study business that he looked for ways to make the money to pay for school. He was good with technology, so he started manufacturing computers and selling them for Rs8,000 a piece. Then he launched into another profit-making venture, printing designs on t-shirts. He managed to get a great client - KLM Airlines. The airline ordered sweatshirts with the KLM emblem and bought in bulk.

Once he made it into his Sales and Marketing class, he met a staunchly radical Hindu young man with a negative opinion of Christians. Abishek noticed one day that the man looked unhappy. He went to him, put his hand on his shoulder and asked, "What has happened?"

"I just lost my father," the young man said. "He was killed in a road accident yesterday. And I don't know how I will continue studying this course." Abishek told him, "We'll work together." From then on, Abishek shared the income from his two businesses, totally paying for his friend's education as well as his own.

After business school, Abishek started a bakery, employing people from the slums as workers. He and his partners, a Christian couple, were committed to running the business with Christian values. It has been very profitable

Along with the bakery, Abishek also started a ministry with street children, renting a house where boys could find shelter at night. Now the boys have a place to get cleaned up, eat an evening meal and participate in Christian activities, get breakfast in the morning, and the opportunity to go to school.

where hard work, diligence, thrift, and integrity are expected. Some disparage such primal faith. My years of experience in the midst of it as confirmed in the literature, indicates it as a powerful source for economic transformation.

Entrepreneurs and Worker Ownership

One entrepreneur called me from Seattle and asked me a question, *Is the small business in the city today the equivalent to the farm in the Jubilee?* For the small business is that which creates wealth. He went on to describe how he had been the entrepreneur behind five businesses. But as he built them he worked to transition the businesses to *worker ownership* and *worker decision-making*. He is not the only one developing this concept.[24] It leads to greater productivity, greater excellence and greater equality.

With our national cultural commitment to egalitarianism, what if New Zealand required all foreign companies to move towards worker ownership as part of the requirements for entry? I know some economists would say that New Zealand already has too high barriers to entry for foreign countries and this would add one more burden. But what if we were known to lead the world in such a concept? Would that morality actually recruit a certain kind of businessman? Workers gaining shares in the company is a first step. The reward for their hard labour is seen in the increase in their shares.

> **Worker Ownership**
>
> Entrepreneurs committed to equality as a goal, need to consider how to progress towards worker ownership and profit sharing.

This principle of *cooperation* is also critical for the rule of thumb that an individual starting a business has a 80% probability of failing within five years, whereas if three people work as a team to form a business with complementary skills, the probability is of 80% success in five years, confirming the Biblical principle of *cooperative work*ing together. These odds can be improved through training in core entrepreneurial skills.

In a later chapter we discuss how revivals and a Christianity of holiness or discipleship and the discipling of national structures are essential elements to the integrity, trust, hard work, creativity needed for a country to produce successful entrepreneurs.

We have reviewed some negatives and some positives of Capitalism through the lenses of ten Christian principles. Those same principles can be applied to a critique of the alternative systems of Socialism and then to the rapid emergence of some more exploitative systems of global Capitalism that are seeking to emerge.

12. Kingdom, Socialist and Marxist Theories

All forms of Socialism share a belief that only through some form of collective organization, some form of collective action, can the individual come nearest to fulfilling his potentialities. Nearly all forms of Socialism have believed that this can best be accomplished only through the elimination of unearned increment, and most of them have insisted on the collective ownership of at least some of the means of production.[1]

Historically, it is impossible to analyse the current global economic world system, without reviewing Socialism. Despite the recognition globally that Communism has universally failed as a philosophy, Socialism remains. We can distinguish between various types of Socialism. **Communism** is characterised by a powerful state which directs the economy by means of central planning. **Neo-Marxist Socialism** has updated the Marxist analysis of Capitalism and seeks to introduce Socialism by a quiet revolution in which the state takes over giant companies and coordinates their activities by a limited planning mechanism, and by strict control of the financial sector. The **social democratic tradition**, rejects Marx' analysis of Capitalism and proposes a Socialism which involves detailed regulation of a capitalist economy, without the abandonment of capitalist firms and enterprises as the basic productive unit.

The extreme forms are Marxist. Marx and Engels in *The Class Struggle* and Marx in other writings, give us some brilliant social analyses and some destructive conclusions. Unlike our time living under Marxism in Kolkata and working alongside Marxists in the slums of Manila, we rarely in New Zealand encounter pure Marxism, but a more moderated form of Global Socialism – at times neo-Marxist in the Labour party and occasionally social democratic in the National Party.

We can also differentiate between the types of organisation made use of by Socialism. This varies from the democratic party type such as we have in New Zealand that looks forward to achieving Socialism by gradual means rather than by sudden revolution, to the *democratic centralism* of state Socialism of the former USSR. The increased trend to legislate public control or ownership in certain economic areas in capitalist societies should not necessarily be interpreted as state Socialism, it is more likely reinforcement of a form of state Capitalism. The National Party of New Zealand would identify itself with such a philosophy not a socialist philosophy.

There are also both Christian and secular attempts to form local communities with common sharing of possessions. Some have identified themselves with socialist agendas. Christian Socialism was a viable alternative in Britain early in the 1900's. But most Christian communities are simply an outworking of Biblical principles in a community. There are also consumer cooperatives, producer cooperatives, trade unions which apply cooperative principles but may or may not be related to overarching socialist agendas.

The Meaning of History

The varieties of Socialism have underlying views of history coming to a culmination. *Christian Socialism* is built on a millennial perspective and a necessary preparation for that millennium, either in separating from the world in separated communities or in engaging in the social problems of all humanity bringing the Kingdom of God now, as a sign of the future Kingdom.

Marxism and the great majority of socialists reject the supernatural and hold a secular belief that the highest human development can and will be reached through historical processes, and this can be accomplished though specific collectivist organisation. Helen Clark, Michael Moore and other socialists within the New Zealand Labour party had links to these values of the global socialist movement.

Attitudes towards Historical Change

The great majority of secular socialists believe that the goal lies in the future, but differ as to the historical methods of reaching this goal. Some insist that history operates through catastrophe and revolution, some have an evolutionary view, some uphold a theory of cyclical repetition. Karl Marx doctrine of dialectical materialism is a combination, for according to the dialectic, any given tendency or *thesis* eventually gives rise to its antithesis, and after a violent struggle – the revolution – a synthesis takes place. *Materialism* represents Marx's commitment to an economic vs a spiritual determinism. Reality is grounded in the social and physical environment.

Marx, living in the era of the enclosures and the creation of massive capitalist-owned factories employing workers for wages, and reflecting on the feudal class struggles of history, understood the meaning of history in terms of class struggle.

> *The history of all hitherto existing society is the history of class struggle – oppressor and oppressed stood in constant opposition to one another... a fight that ended either in revolutionary reconstruction of society or in the common ruin of the contending classes...*

Such struggles would be resolved in the emergence of the *proletariat*, a new class that would overthrow the existing order and replace class struggle with a classless society. In reality, Marxism has resulted in a bureaucracy so corrupt that eventually it has collapsed in European countries under its corruption.

Only from a Christian heritage could Marx have developed these Christian heresies. History indeed has within it a theme of class struggles but it is not this that gives meaning to history. For the Christian, history has meaning as

147

the story of humanity's relationship to God, humanity's relationship to creation and active interventive rule of God in earth. Sometimes God uses class struggles (and I am part of them as I work with slum-dwellers defending their rights to exist), but the scriptures indicate that he dictates his own *when and how* of putting down the mighty and uplifting the poor.

Economic Determinism

For Marx, mankind is shaped by economic forces. Yet the very definition of humanity in the scriptures is that we are distinguished from the animals as soon as we begin to produce our means of subsistence. The economic system drives the way of life. Marx' doctrine of economic determinism, *that the organisation of production is the key to understanding all relationships in society, not least the question of the locus of power, and how that power is exercised*, has infiltrated all of Socialism . This contrasts with the Biblical narrative, particularly with Jesus, who saw the core of life as spiritual, but that spirituality being outworked in social, economic and political dimensions.

Problems of Alienation and Exploitation

Marx would not have followers if some of his analysis did not make sense, touching raw nerves and bringing possible glimmers of hope. He understood the alienation from nature when people are simply cogs in the machinery of production. Similarly, when goods are produced in factories, the role of craftsman, the expression of creativity is alienated. If people become pawns, then social alienation into isolation occurs.[2]

The Class Struggle vs. Peace-making

Marx goes further than this, developing a theory of economic history rising and falling towards revolutions in the means of production.

> *The history of all society up to now is the history of class struggles. Freeman and slave, patrician and plebeian, lord and serf, guildmaster and journeyman, in short, oppressor and oppressed stood in continual conflict with one another, conducting an unbroken, now hidden, now open struggle, a struggle that finished each time with a revolutionary transformation of society as a whole, or with the common ruin of the contending classes*

The Communist Manifesto (Karl Marx & Engels, 1848).

The Bible has more to say on the roles of rich and poor, the causes of riches and poverty; and the judgment of God on the oppressors and uplifting of the oppressed than on many other topics. The earlier word study on poverty or one by Hanks[3] on oppression are most informative.

Marx, like Christians, felt deeply the need to change this poverty. He sees the gradual development of concerted action by the working class as it develops unions, then revolts, riots and eventually revolution as the method of reaching his utopia which is the equality of all men and women. To accomplish this, the revolution has as its mission *to destroy all previous securities and insurances of individual property.*

The scriptures in contrast affirm private ownership and family ownership of property is to be protected. And in contrast with agitating for conflict, the scriptures speak of peace-making as a central motif.

- The peace-maker of the beatitudes is not one who accepts the status quo, but one who strives within the society to bring *shalom.*
- It begins with an understanding of the spirit of the poor, he knows that *blessed are the poor in spirit.*
- He fights for justice because *blessed are those who mourn.*
- And he is one who mourns at the sin and suffering of his people. He has renounced the use of power and force and this can never become Marxist, since *blessed are the meek.*
- Yet he actively involves himself in the struggle to bring truth and justice since *blessed are those who hunger and thirst for righteousness.*
- But this drive for right is balanced with a reconciliatory, redemptive spirit towards those who are perpetuating the wrong since *blessed are the merciful.*
- It is tinged with a selflessness, and seeks nothing for itself since *blessed are the pure in heart.*
- This person is the peace-maker and for this he receives the blessing of persecution from both Marxist and capitalist alike and yet rejoices.[4]

Marxism unleashes forces into the community which it cannot control. Its violence begets violence, just as the injustice of big extremes of wealth involved in the *Linear Take-Off Theory* of Rostow begets further injustice within Capitalism.

Utopia-Equality?

Marx reverts back to his Christian heritage in his search for utopia. Whether equality is the aim of the scriptures or not is a debatable issue. Certainly there is an equalising and a passion for equity. Jesus and the Gospel are certainly levellers. James, his brother, speaking of the effects of the Kingdom, tells us, *Let the lowly brother boast in his exaltation and the rich in his humiliation.*[5]

Paul uplifts the slave-master relationship to that of brothers, following Jesus teaching to *call no-one master, or teacher, or father, since you are all brothers.*[6] Social status and barriers are destroyed in the gospel. All men and women are of equal and infinite worth in God's sight. All are called to become their brother's servants.

Economic differences are also to some extent equalised. In the early church they had all the things in common, some sold their possessions and others shared what they had.[7] These practices continue today in many Christian groups.

Abraham, David, Daniel were rich and godly. Alternatively, Zacheus, when confronted with Jesus, knew that he must act *Lord half my goods I give to the poor.*[8] Few Christians surrounded by poverty can stay rich when the scripture say, *if anyone has this worlds goods and sees his brother in need, yet closes his heart against him, how does God's love abide in him.*[9]

While there is no force involved in these changes in the New Testament, when we examine the Jubilee we see a statement of a Political Economy with enforced redistribution. The New Testament model stems freely from transformed value systems and there is a gentle acceptance of those who have not reached this degree of commitment.

The utopia of the scriptures is something that we can seek to build here on earth within communities of believers but only imperfectly. Expanding the principles of Jubilee, we should seek it more broadly within society – but it does not look like Marx's Utopia, particularly the practice of Stalin's or Mao's murderous progressions towards utopia and the bureaucratic results. It will only be fulfilled on that day when the new heaven and the new earth are revealed.

Our utopia is in the symbolism of John's Revelation, of the new heavens and new earth.

- It is a place where God dwells
- It is a place without pain or death
- It will have all it needs for life
- It will be filled with a sense of heritage and belonging
- There will be no murderers, rapists, liars, etc. there. It will be internally peaceful.

The holy city will be perfectly built, brilliantly designed and spacious.

- It will be well protected and exceedingly rich
- It will be full of many cultures
- It will be clean
- Its plants will always be fruitful
- It will bring healing to the nations.

Read it in all its poetry in Revelation 21. This is what we seek to bring on earth, knowing it will be but imperfect. We hold a hope of its fulfilment beyond the earth in a new heavens and a new earth. Marx caught but an economic inkling of this reality.

The Biblical View of Property

All economic systems are based on ownership of property. The view of property ownership in both Socialism and Capitalism conflict with the biblical view of property:

> *The land shall not be sold in perpetuity, for the land is mine, for you are merely my tenants and share croppers.*[10]

God owns the land: men and women do not have inviolable property rights, nor does the Government own the land. However each family that was released from the slavery of Egypt was given an inheritance and this remained. Every fifty years it was returned to the original owners if it has been sold. So we see a pattern of periodic land reforms and equalisation.

The value of land has to do with its production. Communism with its government-ownership of all land certainly destroys this heritage. Since Communism's fall, the rejection of this form of state ownership has in practice negated this tenet. Yet so does Capitalism destroy this heritage, as rich men and women acquire more and more land that belongs by heritage to their brothers. British Capitalism was built on the enclosures when the feudal Lords took control of the commons violating a thousand years of mutual contact between Lord and peasant. The resultant migration of millions from Britain to the New World, Australia, New Zealand and South Africa was a desperate search for land.

Changing Structures – Violence?

Marxism errs also in its methodology of changing structures. Much of liberation theology coming out of South America follows the same error. The arguments go something like this.

- The men and women in power are corrupt. Therefore:
- The structures are corrupt, therefore:
- We must change the structures
- It must be done quickly, radically

The 2nd step is logical since structures are webs of relationships institutionalised. The third is also logical but incomplete. It should read, "We must change the structures by changing corruption into righteousness," since to replace corrupt men and women with corrupt men and women only creates another web of institutionalised corrupt relationships.

There are two ways to change the corrupt men and women and their corrupt structures. One is to reconcile them also to submission to the Kingdom of God by preaching the gospel in the context of living out the role of prophet, or peacemaker, or priest or suffering servant.

The second is to replace the men and women in power with new men and women. Here Christians in their struggle to establish the Kingdom of God, part ways again with their Marxist friends as to methodology for Romans 13 tells us:

> *Let every person by subject to the governing authorities. For there is no authority except from God, and those that exist have been instituted by God. Therefore he who resists the authorities resists what God has appointed, and those who resist will incur judgment...*

This was written under an oppressive, exploitative, right-wing Roman government and clearly reflects the Old Testament teachings on respect for authority. David refused to kill King Saul for Saul was God's anointed.[11] *It is God who executes judgment, putting down one and lifting up another.*[12] So we are commanded,

> *Beloved, never avenge yourself, since it is written "Vengeance is mine, I will repay", says the Lord. No, if your enemy is hungry feed him. If he is thirsty give him drink.*[13]

Our commitment to structural change is the same, but our methodology is the opposite of the Marxists. Our methodology will bring in harmony between people. Our methodology is the lived-out Sermon on the Mount and the proclamation of the gospel that reconciles peoples within evil colonialism, cultural imperialism and oppressive governments.

We say no to violence, no to oppression, no to injustice and we say that the antidote to all violence is aggressive peace-making; to all hatred is love; to abusive use of power is servanthood.

Within these Christian values, the resistance and aggressive peace-making requires organisation. It requires organizing the power of numbers of the people against the power of the wealthy oppressors and their lawyers and political influence. And that organizing is built on an understanding of truth in the situation. Thus the role of the academics, the journalists, the media remains critical. When we do this within Capitalist societies, then the possibility of being labelled Marxist is high, as these words are slogans. We are not Marxist, we are simply Christians seeking to work against the unjust exercise of power.[14]

Sustaining the public space where such power struggles and outing of truth can occur, is essential. Within Marxism, that public space is destroyed. Truth becomes subservient to the Party, not the people. However, within capitalist New Zealand, we also need to protect that public space. In my opinion, and most differ, one of the worst losses we faced as a people was the abolishing of the upper house of the New Zealand parliament. While imperfect, costly and at times laughable, it provided checks and balances on the power of government. With its abolishment, each party has swung from one extreme to the other, without accountability, except the ballot box but that is fragile as often the opposition parties are splintered, so no threat at the ballot.

But ultimately, our meekness will win, our cause will succeed. Since our time frame is eternal. We serve a God who is gracious and patient, who waits for oppressors to repent.[15] So we do no lose hope despite our chosen powerlessness and suffering servant role. On that day we will be justified.

Eventually, if economic systems do not voluntarily apply principles of the Jubilee, the gap between rich and poor escalates exponentially. As the cries of the poor reach up to the Lord of hosts, the system itself faces judgement.. Marx prophesied the increasing oscillations of the Capitalist system till eventually it collapsed. While his solutions were horrific, often his analysis was accurate. One wonders if the next oscillation of the global economic system might be that crash.

13. Discipling the Global Economy

An isle is emerging that is bigger than a continent - the Interlinked Economy (ILE) of the triad (the United States, Europe, and Japan), joined by aggressive economies such as Taiwan, Hong Kong and Singapore... It will encompass most East European countries, most of the Asian newly industrialised economies, and some Latin American countries.

It is becoming so powerful that it has swallowed most consumers and corporations, made traditional national borders almost disappear, and pushed bureaucrats, politicians, and the military toward the status of declining industries.

The ILE has a resident body of approximately 1 billion people, enjoying on average $10,000 per capita gross national product. It is in the ILE that most of the wealth in the world is created, consumed and redistributed...

The Borderless World: Power and Strategy in the Interlinked Economy

Kenichi Ohmae

Traditional Economics in a Global Economy

Our responsibility, given by Jesus, is to disciple the nations, that is, to bring their people, structures and culture under the authority of his Kingdom. This includes Kingdom conflict with existing "isms" or philosophies. While some speak of spiritual warfare as shouting out against these, Paul prefers to combat these false philosophies in public debate.[1] The realm of scholarship is thus the primary context of changing the spirituality of nations. Such scholarship is an intensely spiritual discipline and we need to encourage many to engage it with serious passion.

In the economic sphere, that involves affirming philosophies that build from Kingdom principles and combatting false economic philosophies. While economics is based on theories and is academic in formulation, politics is based on issues, so we need also to engage the political economic issues of the day, a very different style.

We can begin with affirmation of global trade as a lifeline that has enabled New Zealand to sustain a high level of living over the decades, by implementing principles of *creativity, productivity,* and *good management* in ways that have served the living standard of the whole nation.

In the 1980's, when I was first studying development economics in Manila, predictions were being made as to the coming world controlled by the multinationals. I had a question that has sat in the back of my minds as to how these multinationals will not only wrest economic but also legal and political controls from nation-states. How could autocratic boardrooms dispossess our democratic nation. Clearly there would need to be collusion with one set of politicians or another, but we have seen how fickle such ruling clusters are. So there would have to be more. We examine that in this chapter.

Pakeha Christians (and I am one), were largely oppressed, dispossessed peasants in England, Scotland and Ireland, who fought for freedom from oppression and migrated to New Zealand to build a land of the free.

Beginning with roots in Capitalism but coming from the dispossessed poor, we crafted a society built on justice, well influenced by the ethics of early Methodist leaders, and then by the Labour movement, in creating what much of the democratised world has moved to – *a mixed economy*; built on freedom, sustained by Capitalism, socialised in its redistribution of wealth. Michael Novak calls it Democratic Capitalism. The government regulates and manages some of the free economy. It also is directly involved in economic activity. Capitalism without governmental intrusion cannot provide housing for the poor, effective policing, social security, education, cultural and social welfare, reconciliation, highways, parks, national security.

But the Labour government of the 1990's sold New Zealand's bank assets, forestry assets, land assets and housing assets (Kelsey, 2015). This was part of an era called *neoliberalism* among academics and economists. The argument was made that it was necessary to sustain the education, the welfare, the pension systems. We all face such logic at times -when we face a cash flow situation, should we sell some assets? In the week before taking power it became clear that the previous Prime Minister, Robert Muldoon has nearly bankrupted the country. Urgent action had to be taken, including devaluation and asset sales.

Margaret Thatcher, prime minister of England, was the cover girl of the magazines for divesting her government of assets, and New Zealand Labour followed her pathway with a vengeance. But as our people having gained our freedom from British oppression, why would we now put ourselves under the jurisdiction of foreign banks? Most of us during those years were shell-shocked by what happened. Jane Kelsey describes the sale of most of the 14 New Zealand banks to foreign banks. *By 1995, fourteen of New Zealand's sixteen registered banks were entirely or substantially foreign owned.*[2] Since their profits go to shareholders that means a percentage each year of all of New Zealand's banking profits goes overseas. Jim Anderton's formation of Kiwibank, owned by Kiwis, was a wise response but not enough to regain what had been lost.

Since then, New Zealand has continued to stagger in its responses to globalisation. But the times are complex, so perhaps our leadership are owed some grace. Most statistics and economic theories are based on the national model of the closed economy. These models can be evaluated against the ethics of the Kingdom. However, this becomes more complex as the rapid expansion of technological innovation, communications and the global economy throws conventional economics into confusion:

- **Global job markets**: An accelerating national economy may not produce more jobs. Jobs may be created abroad.
- **Role of central banks:** The instruments of central bankers - interest rate and money supply are made obsolete. If interest rates rise, cheaper funds may flow in from abroad.
- **Speculation:** Interest bearing instruments have taken a back seat to non-interest bearing (and often speculative) instruments such as real estate, stocks, and currency exchange markets.
- **Technology creating invisibility:** The flow of funds is largely invisible, as production and other functions can be moved between countries.
- **Wealth creation:** Wealth is now largely created on paper in the marketplace, rather than in the real world of the soils that contain natural resources.
- **Security through interdependence**: Interdependence of economies creates security. That will be the governing mindset rather than military-based security.
- People become **global consumers** when they have access to information about people and services from around the world.
- **Resource wars:** Resources such as water, oil, minerals will become increasingly scarce globally generating resource wars in multiple contexts.[3]
- **Escalating buying of real estate:** China and richer Middle Eastern economies are now buying large tracts of land, mineral rights and buying governments and their UN votes through "aid" projects.[4] Since the 1970's much of the seabeds also have now rapidly been claimed.[5]
- **Competing trade alliances:** In the Pacific, this is part of a trade war between China and the United States. Both are working furiously to set up their own alliances.
- **Technological globalisation**: the speed of change of technology requires rapidly changing responses.

Most of the above involve ethical issues. Thus, we have to discern the ethical issues, not only of New Zealand economics but the economic global interfaces. This is not a spiritual work for the faint-hearted. Even for economists it is no simple feat. Clusters of Christians (for it is of necessity a group task involving theological and economic input) wishing to engage in evaluating national economics against the morality of the Kingdom has to "discern" (a classic term in Christian spirituality) both the global economic principles and how these measure up against Biblical norms.

Prophecy and an Integrated World Economy

This often leaves us as lone voices against the flow. And unwelcome moral voices. The difficulty in New Zealand is where are those moral voices? Who is willing to stand? And stand alone? While writing this, I put one critique of Capitalism up on my Facebook. It resulted in more responses than a year of other Facebook posts about the needs of the poor. Only four of them responding on track to the issue. So who wants to get that kind of barrage of angry people and public debate?

Such public Christian voices need to be informed by an eschatology, an understanding of the climax of history in the books of Daniel and Revelations. Throughout Christian history, and particularly since the end of nineteenth century students of biblical prophecy have been attentive to the concept of the emergence of one world government based on an economic unity that has totalitarian control.[6]

It is typed as "Babylon".[7] Erudite French philosopher-theologian Ellul's classic *Meaning of the City,* tracks this theme of Babylon, the "City of Man" as against Jerusalem, the "City of God", throughout the scriptures. While during the days of the writer, John the apostle, this referred to Rome, as with much prophecy there is also a future meaning related to the latter days. This globalised civilisation extending the Roman system and economy will require complete submission. It will include political, economic and religious control of an absolute nature. Membership will be strictly obtained through a mark imprinted on hand or forehead. It will be based in Europe.[8] Based on these passages alone, Christians are led into an opposition to the emergence of a globally interlinked economy.

Survival by believers opposing the emergence of a global unified world economic, religious and governmental system will require specific attention to maintaining privacy from government entities, separation from its religious admixture[9] and result for many in martyrdom.[10]

The destruction by God of this coming integrated global economic, political, religious global urban society, will usher in the millennial reign of Christ. There are numerous interpretations of how this will happen, such that we are wary of being dogmatic, but whichever we hold, we are commanded in the meantime to be watchful, to be holy, to be separated from the values and culture that is emerging.

A motivating factor to engage in such struggles is that our works here within God's purposes, will not be burned up but be honoured into his millennial reign. Such eternal work perhaps includes creation of alternative economic systems built on the principles of the Kingdom of God in the present.

Fatal Ethical Flaws in Global Capitalism

The near collapse of the US system and hence global capitalist system in 2008 has unmasked the Powers behind such a system in an unusual way. Two historical processes have been foundational to the present dilemmas.

1. The development of central banks (based on the model of the *Reichsbank* of Germany)

2. These began the development of an asset-based currency based on human debts and obligations instead of a currency based on gold and silver values related to actual resource production.

3. This dissociation has enabled governments to consistently print new money, which since the 1940's has created ongoing inflationary economies.

4. Each year in OECD nations, governments spend beyond their income and both increase taxation levels and produce paper money to cover this extra expense.

The Genesis of Global Economic Slavery

How did a few banking organisations gain such control over decisions related to finances? The success of the central banking scheme developed into a far-reaching plan described by President Clinton's mentor, Georgetown Professor Carroll Quigley,

> *To create a world system of financial control in private hands able to dominate the political system of each country and the economy of the world as a whole. This system was to be controlled in a feudalist fashion by the central banks of the world acting in concert, by secret agreements arrived at in frequent meetings and conferences. The apex of the system was to be the* Bank for International Settlements in Basel, Switzerland, *a private bank owned and controlled by the world's central banks which were themselves private corporations. Each central bank.... sought to dominate its government by its ability to control Treasury loans, to manipulate foreign exchanges, to influence the levels of economic activity in the country, and to influence cooperative politicians by subsequent economic rewards in the business world.*

Given such a critique, can one affirm this development? It has enabled some decades of global economic growth for many countries, during which time, over thirty countries have moved from poverty to significant wealth. And many millions have moved out of poverty.

Is that because of these centralised systems? Those involved in them and benefiting from them would honour them. To suggest that they have been carriers of our ten Biblical principles released through the reformation into the creation of economic theory and structures would not be unreasonable, but would be laughed at by many skilled in development economics. To suggest that other principles of greed, centralisation of control, exploitation of people and resources have been built into these structures would be affirmed by most academics, and rejected by politicians and bankers.

One of the evils at root to this system of this interconnected system of national banks is the process of money creation. One of the benefits is how after the 2008 crash, the *Bank of International Settlements* has imposed limits on the ratio of money banks can produce to their actual capital. This currently is 8% rising to 10.5% by 2019 (there are many complexities to these figures).[11]

Mike Moore, famous as a New Zealander heading the World Trade Organization, describes his own pilgrimage into globalisation because of his commitment to universal values, solidarity, unity and tolerance. One of his applications of those commitments was in enabling smaller nations to enter into global trade discussions of the WTO. He saw the creation of global rules for free trade as mechanisms that have created freedom for millions, and benefitted life expectancy, infant mortality, literacy, access to clean water, democracy and human rights.[12] New Zealand governments, both Labour and National have followed that same line of thinking and continue to confirm that TTPA is a rational and good extension of those values.

Biblical Perspectives on Global Economic Powers

Which of the above analyses of globalisation is correct? how as New Zealand Christians do we apply these ten Biblical principles at global levels to seek to determine that?

Our Biblical critique started with our simple principles, but touches the core of these global processes: the lust for things, and pride in our possessions are an endemic part of a moral depravity that perverts the basics of a sound economic system of allocation. This is not from the Father. The Bible calls this *greed* - a perverted use of resources for selfish ends. Inherent in the ideal of *regulated* Capitalism, this also becomes manifest as a societally mandated perversion. Scriptures indicate that such greed brings a curse. A curse on human relationships to land, a curse on the land itself, a curse on production, a curse on meaning and time.

At national and international levels, recognition of greed as the driver of Capitalism a theme that predated Adam Smith, but often carries his name, requires regulation, or the rich will continue to get richer, and the poor, poorer. It also requires periodic redistribution and equalisation as modelled in the principles of the Jubilee (though we should never seek to impose the specifics).

Thus beyond prophetic denunciation of evils within every system is the necessity for Christians to create accountability within these systems for equity, redistribution and *pushing decisions down from global to local economic development*, rather than allowing increasingly centralised processes of control, now accelerating as computerisation exponentially increases capacities for control. Jesus conflict with lawyers and politicians sometimes gives me pause to think. They inhabit the pinnacles of power globally. We must *push decision-making down to the people* and away from those pinnacles of power as an essential principle of empowerment of the people and disempowerment of the 1%.

The Christian process of doing this is not revolutionary, but evolutionary, seeking change at myriads of points. This is the classic model Jesus taught to all Christians to be salt, silently impacting society and keeping it from rot (as against the revolutionary model of cataclysmic change). However, if this approach fails and oppression runs unchecked, the scriptures – and history – are replete with examples of God himself stepping in and judging nations, cities, empires at devastating asymptotic collapse.

At a prophetic level, the scriptures call us to confront the Principalities and Powers behind the 'isms' of the day.[13] In relationship to Global Capitalism there are many points where New Zealanders need to fight to protect their culture and resources, as increasingly companies, land and resources are being sold to international interests, so that the production of the land benefits foreigners. (Larger nations can print more money and enforce global contracts to the benefit of their larger economies without respect for smaller nations and local communities).

Fortunately, until now, in New Zealand, we have had reasonable public space where debate on such issues can be freely pursued. Though those who are vocal come under pressure from those in power, such as the SIS investigations of Jane Kelsey, who has written against globalisation. And we need not be naïve - members of the New Zealand government are increasingly beholden to the UN, World Bank, and IMF agendas, which are not determined by the people of New Zealand.

Survival in a Geo-Political Economic War?

Currently, under the guise of free trade, a very different agenda is being advanced within the TPPA agreement , to extend foreign access to New Zealand's assets. While New Zealand was part of the original mooting of the ideal of a structured, high quality free trade deal along with Singapore, Chile and Brunei, the US and Japan have largely set the agenda for this deal. In our search for better access to the US market, an always elusive goal for NZ, are we giving away too much? Having gained our freedom over centuries, why would we now put ourselves under the jurisdiction of American agendas and law?

The Chinese are not far behind in trying to create their own trade bloc. Using "aid" they have been placing themselves in a position with many small countries globally, including the Pacific Islands, to control votes in the UN and other international bodies. They are rapidly buying up resources across Africa and land in many countries. So an economic and political war for resources between the world's two largest economies is being played out in the name of Free Trade.

Free trade is a commonly known economic concept that as a nation we have committed to and it has largely been to our benefit as a small trading nation with a highly skilled workforce. Essentially, there is solid research that if nations mutually drop tariffs on imported goods, both trading partners are likely to increase the amount of trade and both will do better. This goes back to a comparison three centuries ago between Britain and France. Britain opened its borders to trade. France closed them with tariffs. Britain's economy grew, France faced shortages.

Over time, this historic idea has morphed because of another economic idea of *competitive advantage*. In each country there are some goods that country can produce more efficiently, either because of raw materials or manpower skills. If each country focusses their trading on those areas where they have this competitive advantage, both will profit.[14] Thus in establishing free trade with China before any other nation, Labour Prime Minister, Helen Clark, knew the clothing and shoe industries would disappear in New Zealand as factories were unable to compete with low wage production in China. The theory is that the workers in these industries would move to higher productive industries, which we would then export to China to New Zealand's advantage. An argument can be made that overall, New Zealand likely benefitted from such an agreement with the open doors to China.

But there are complications with this theory. The rise of Chinese low wage, low price exports largely caused the number of jobs in the apparel industry in the US to drop from 840,000 to 118,000 between 1990 to 2010.[15] No amount of retraining could recover these. Financial bubbles can form where small countries are overwhelmed by deficits. Single product island states are subject to an imbalance of trade. Agriculturally-based societies such as New Zealand continue to grow exports at rates determined by natural growth. But industrial products that are imported increase in costs far more rapidly, creating an imbalance of trade. *Fair trade* is a wiser approach for smaller nations.

With TPPA, we are facing a seismic ethical economic shift. At the centre of this was the US loss of control of the global WTO (World Trade Organization) negotiations (in the 2008 Doha round) when Brazil, and India, who are now significant global economies, identified alternative agendas. The consultations ended in deadlock and confusion.

At the same time, a massive trade war is emerging between the US and China, with these emergent powers, the BRICS (Brazil, Russia, India and China, which are all deemed to be at a similar stage of newly advanced economic development), in China's orbit.

The TPP is an expansion of the Trans-Pacific Strategic Economic Partnership Agreement (TPSEP or P4) signed by Brunei, Chile, New Zealand, and Singapore in 2005. In 2008, others joined and the US began to dominate processes as it developed a new strategy of developing three regional trade agreements. These are informed by significant involvement of 600 US multinationals at the core of influence on the TPPA negotiations – and no trade unions, no civil society organisations that might represent the voice of the people, the voice of democracy.

It is a gigantic strategy by the US to rewrite the rules of the global economy and control global decision-making outside of nation-state legal systems, with the dominance of the largest US global corporations.

The US have put in place a grand military enclosure of China in the Pacific. This was overt with Hillary Clinton's visit to NZ as Secretary of State. They are now seeking to put a grand global economic enclosure of 2/3 of the worlds GDP, and 61 nations. There are three regional trade agreements in process: TISA in Europe, TTIP across the Atlantic, TTPA around the Pacific. They exclude the BRIC's.[16]

Abrogation of Democracy

Trade may benefit from negotiations behind closed doors but democracies do not prosper in the dark.

Many voices reflecting years of development studies research indicate that these are a major threat to our democracy, and our independence as a nation. I personally have tracked with that research over the decades, so the opposition makes perfect sense. The complexity is that as a nation that affirms free trade, New Zealand has been the enthusiastic catalyst of this process, but these agreements are not just about trade, but have become much more.

The initial point of anger of thousands across the Pacific nations and in the US was the secrecy of the agreements being drafted. Through Wikileaks and other leaks, parts of the agreement became public. In November 2015, a draft was released publicly for New Zealand (Ministry of Foreign Affairs and Trade, 2015). Of particular offense is that once they have been revealed, governments have to vote for the whole package, not piece by piece, as is standard best practice in democratic governmental law-making. Trade may benefit from negotiations behind closed doors but democracies certainly do not prosper in the dark.

The second difficulty is that they are about more than free trade. They impinge on the liberty of the New Zealand people to define and legislate our own health, property ownership, education laws. Thirdly, they set up arbitration courts outside national legal frameworks where corporations may bring court cases against national governments for loss of future profits. (they do not allow for governments to bring court cases against the multinationals). Phillip Morris has already done this against Australia for banning certain cigarette marketing based on a similar earlier agreement.

Fourthly, they will have a dramatic roll-back on environmental progress over the last decades, as governmental changes in laws that preclude multinational corporations from damaging the environment are challengeable in extra-judicial global courts. This is not the opinion of fringe activists. In an open letter from 400 environmental leaders to the US Congress , June 9, 2016, the following defines the core issues:

> *However, two pending trade deals pose major barriers to this climate imperative. The Trans-Pacific Partnership (TPP) and the Transatlantic Trade and Investment Partnership (TTIP), as proposed, would empower an unprecedented number of fossil fuel corporations, including some of the world's largest polluters, to challenge U.S. policies in tribunals not accountable to any domestic legal system. There, the firms could use the trade pacts' broad foreign investor rights to demand compensation for U.S. fossil fuel restrictions. These "investor-state dispute settlement" (ISDS) cases would be decided not by judges, but by lawyers who typically represent corporations.*[17]

Jane Kelsey, as a dedicated academic, with years of expertise on international trade and development issues, has been a prophetic voice of opposition on these issues and many others related to this agreement. Despite being pilloried by government ministers, she reflects the mainstream critiques of the international development community, and some of the theories examined in the chapter critiquing Capitalism but now applied to this present issue. Other similar responses can be found on the *Its Our Future* web site.[18]

If we apply our ten principles to this agreement some would find them affirming the agreement. But we find some serious violations of the divine order in favour of the multinational world (US?) order.

- In May 2016, a US government department has come out with an independent analysis indicating that it would not significantly increase trade for the US. Non-governmental comments on analysis in NZ is saying the same. So it fails the *productivity* test.

- As one who has sought to gain trademarks both in NZ and the US, its imposition of US copyright and trademarking processes are chilling. There are many concluding it will hinder the world of the *creative* NZ artist. Having attempted to trade mark and copyright products in both the US and New Zealand, any intrusion of US-style approaches to copyright would be a great hindrance to New Zealand's efficiency and very costly in legal fees.

> **Incremental Legislation**
>
> Governments have to vote for the whole TPPA package, not piece by piece, as is best practice in democratic law-making.

- There is little attention to principles of *equity, equality, redistribution* within the process or what is known of its framework, nor affirmation of nation – states being required to prefer such principles over against profit-making by global corporations. Workers Unions were not included in its framing, nor those schooled in international development thinking with its emphasis on the voice of the people.

- While NZ may have an increased possibility of access for its imports to the US, all of our former discussion about the *end goals of wealth creation* and the nature of the Kingdom of God become subject to US defined economic goals. In short, the agreement appears to allow the corporate world to define the parameters for social goals, an *economic determinism* that ultimately undermines socio-political realities.

- Arbitration of disputes is given to courts under no national or international jurisdiction. Large corporations may sue national governments at the costs of tens of millions of dollars for possible lost income based on governments preferring changes in law to accomplish social objectives. This is an *economic determinism*, that we see violates principles of the *holistic* Kingdom of God that balances social responsibility, environmental responsibility and economic aims.

Based on such discussions, I would suggest Christians, while affirming *fair trade*, need to be at the forefront of opposition by a small country such as New Zealand to any agreement like this, largely determined by an empire and global multinationals, utilising the phrase *free trade* to hide a very different set of agendas of lifting national governmental freedoms to define social responsibilities that limit ownership. There is no opportunity, once signed to opt out of provisions. While there may be pride in having initiated the negotiations, it does not mean New Zealand should ratify it.

Other Christians may take these same Biblical principles and based on the government's analysis, conclude that this agreement will increase *productivity*, open markets, and as such benefit not just New Zealand but other countries, and that threats to our sovereignty are overstated by fringe elements. Free trade brings about greater *equity* between nations. With Mike Moore, a champion of the labouring man, as our voice as Director-General of the WTO for many years, and as a prime mover behind the DOHA round of negotiations, NZ has had a vested interest in the development of global free trade processes. There is value in continuing to be seen at the forefront (But not value in being seen to be duped by larger nations).

Either way, we need to propose alternative *fair trade* as against free trade agreements that are *derived from the people's perspectives*. But more than that, we need to do so in such a way that our hard fought national identity and *democratic freedoms* are not impinged on by foreign powers and arbitration courts not accountable to our political processes.

Which raises a question I (and it seems no one) cannot answer, "what are the alternatives?" We can prophetically critique and resist evils within an agreement such as this as a normative part of our Christian prophetic role. We can affirm an alternative set of ideals such as fair trade vs. free trade. But this route of fair trade has not provided a solid alternative. It has tinkered around the edge of global trade, in a significant way, affecting millions, but nevertheless, not significantly affected the core issues of the global institutionalisation of free trade in a rapidly technologically changing world.

Fair trade has become a globally recognized process with its own Federations and standards. Organizations use five tools to contribute to development:

- **Price premiums**. Fair trade products are sometimes priced higher than others. Part of the difference is ploughed back into producer communities in order to improve working conditions.
- **Certification and labelling.** Standards aim to improve product quality, working conditions, environmental sustainability, business development and training.

- **Microcredit** helps small-scale producers get started on fair trade projects.
- **Technical** support includes business development, trade information, advice on quality standards, training in new techniques, etc.
- **Advocacy** is an important element in fair trade marketing, with the branding and fair trade message found on virtually every package.

Fair-traders point out these development advantages:

- Producers get a decent living, gain necessary skills and knowledge, obtain access to credit, find technical assistance and market information, learn about trade and acquire experience in exporting.
- Better prices for farmers do not increase consumer costs, since the fair trade organizations cut out intermediaries by handling all the operations between production and retailing themselves.
- Consumers get an educational tool promoting thoughtful consumerism.[19]

This has worked for coffee, handicrafts and other products that unskilled poor labourers can produce. But only 20% of consumers at a maximum seem ready to pay more for fair trade products in wealthy countries. This limits possible expansion. It is not a comprehensive process replacing other trade dynamics. But it does demonstrate potential pathways forward that support the *principles of equity, equality, and redistribution*, while extending processes of *cooperation, ownership, production and creativity*.

It is obviously a great public humiliation for a NZ Prime Minster to declare opposition to negotiations of which NZ was a charter contributor, and which possibly advance some of our trade interests. But we must fight prophetically against the intrusion of TPPA into our culture as Christians. It at least needs to be sent back for review by environmental groups, workers organizations, and first peoples of nations, and be open to step by step public debate, not a ramming through the political processes.

That still gives some models and principles to build from, but still leaves a conundrum as to what are the alternatives after defeating TPPA. How does the global community build global ethical infrastructure at the postmodern global trading level? The fear that President Obama is using is that if this is not passed, China will step in with its own alternative trade treaties.

As part of my field of urban leadership, in urban economics, Jane Jacob's work[20] on global cities gives one key to how New Zealand should move forward. When cities of equal size begin to trade with each other, the collective processes uplift the income of all. This is in contrast with seeking access to trade with the centres of empire which invariably profit the empire not the smaller city/country. This was significant in the initial attempts by Chile, New Zealand, Malaysia, and Singapore towards fair trade. Subsequently, it appears that such a process has been derailed by the US, Japan and 600 multinationals. Such would be part of an appropriate ministerial statement of withdrawal from TPPA.

Thirdly, applying the principle of *cooperation and equity*, which also are represented in democratic process, to restart such negotiations at the level with equal partner states in size, but inclusive of environmental, trade union, workers groups along with the business community seems an essential element in balancing *social responsibility, economic sharing and increase of productivity* in trade. This might most easily be accomplished if New Zealand was to work with ASEAN, the confederation of states in South East Asia.

The failure to politely withdraw and renegotiate according to principles of justice, would perhaps lead to the similar tensions faced by Brexit, between the disenfranchised populace of New Zealand and the 1% represented by Prime Minister, John Keys and the investment banking community.

14. Economic Discipleship in Action

This study has developed a very simple Biblical theology of ten principles of economics, from surveying themes from Genesis to Revelations. These we have applied at personal, family and community levels initially.

The principle of *ownership* (9) was applied to land issues, which have a particular history in New Zealand. The principle of *management* (8) was applied to the expansion of usury through expanding credit card usage. The principles of *cooperation* (4) led to very different approaches to business formation than are popularized by the markets. The principles of *creativity* (2), *management* (8) and *cooperation* (4) were applied to the emergence of entrepreneurs. These were highlighted by reference to the progressions that have been demonstrated in enabling the urban poor globally to escape poverty. These indicate the importance of expanding alternative banking, housing and insurance *cooperative models* owned by the people of New Zealand. The current discussions on forestry cooperatives possibly bear promise in this regard of regaining control on national assets and productivity.

The application of these principles became increasingly complex in the third section of this book as we reviewed political economic systems: Capitalism, Marxism, Socialism and the mixed economy. They became a critical foundation for then engaging with the sale of *ownership* (9) of New Zealand's essential assets. These same principles lead to a clear call for Christians to oppose the present attempts of the American government with its linkages to multinationals in modifying the TPPA discussions. While New Zealand was a prime mover, the process appears to subvert the autonomy of our government as a *free* people (10), and subvert environmental advances in the name of a very positive ideal, that of free trade. As such, it would appear advisable for New Zealand to reject this deal in favour of renewed negotiations based on fair trade, our commitments to democracy and environmental values.

The final step in a *Transformational Conversation* is to examine the action steps in which the conversation leads us to engage and the structural vehicles to enable these. The following are some suggestions:

Economic Justice for the Poor

Significantly, within the frameworks discussed, is a call to structure economic development in such a way that the dispossessed are empowered economically with work, opportunity and markets. Back in 1981, I wrote core values for establishing the mission *Servants to Asia's Urban Poor*.[1] Those prophetic words have guided those who have walked with us in founding multiple missions, apostolic orders, non-profits, educational programs training now hundreds of workers among the poor.

Called to be peacemakers, where possible, we will seek justice with equity in order to prevent continued political and economic violence and oppression against the poor. We will seek to live in harmony with all men, but in seeking peace will be involved in reflecting the just nature of God into the structures of society in such a way as to speak out for, defend and uplift the poor. We will act in such areas by being wise as serpents and harmless as doves, seeking to effect change by bringing repentance and reconciliation, though this at times may involve us in non-violent confrontations with those who oppress or exploit the poor.

We will seek to avoid social dislocation by encouraging evangelism and development in such a way that the Kingdom of God affects whole communities. A primary focus is the encouragement of technically trained and economically independent church leadership among movements of poor people's churches.

Our commitments are to Biblical justice and equity and hence we renounce the demonic in both Capitalism and Marxist Socialism with their deifying of wealth.

We recognise that the freedoms of democratic Capitalism have enabled the most significant uplift of the poor in history because of its rewards for productivity through profits. Free market economies also are more compatible with Biblically-based concepts of the freedom of the individual than other state-controlled economies. But we seek to develop, modify and bring justice into existing systems by our renunciation of anti-biblical presuppositions inherent in Capitalism of values of greed, excessive profit, usurious interest, the exploitation and dehumanisation of a person as a machine, and the exhausting of irreplaceable natural resources.

We renounce the use of force, violence, the inaccuracy of class struggle analysis, the implied concept of zero-growth equality and the bitterness of Marxism.

We renounce the centralisation of power in elites as being contrary to Biblical principle, either power of an economic Capitalist elite or of a political socialist elite. We work rather for cooperative patterns of development with power diffused as much as possible to local community leadership, recognizing that the multiplication of small grass-roots economic, political and spiritual organisations aids in the diffusion of power, uplift of the poor and protection of freedoms within a nation. While for specific goals we may find ourselves aligned with various political groups, we are committed to none but the politics of the Kingdom of God based on principles of brotherhood, service and accountable freedoms.

We seek to bring biblical values of justice and equity also into the international arena of the usurious international banking and trade systems.

In the intervening decades, while global economic structures have facilitated billions of people in exiting destitution, they have escalated the levels of oppression of other billions. The above words hold as true today as when I wrote them in 1981, thirty-five years ago.

Resisting Evils within Globalisation

So what are areas of response for New Zealand Christians and 4,500 churches to these global changes affecting New Zealand's economics? The following suggestions are a smorgasbord of ideas to explore. We need to be simultaneously involved both in prophetic opposition and activist change *and* in governmental leadership of systems of global economics. For some, it is in opposition to power, for some it is working from the centre of structures – just as Daniel and Isaiah were prophets within the elites, while Amos and Jonah railed from outside the establishment.

Preaching leadership

We first need leadership through moral pastoral preaching, Sunday by Sunday, that is, theological leadership. This should result in congregational discussion as to the nature of engagement in the political and economic processes in a free society as an expression of Biblical truth. I am unaware of any theological course in New Zealand engaging theology with economics. So how do we prepare our pastors? I offer one online as part of the MA in Transformational Urban Leadership.

Given that our Baptist, Methodist, and Presbyterian forefathers fought for such freedom of speech and the value of each individual in governance, I would suggest it would be ungodly for the Christian and evangelical churches not to engage.

But there is also a historical background of non-engagement in the structures of society, by these churches who were formed in opposition to the Anglican, Presbyterian and Catholic state churches. These were formed in revivals, this being an essential element of the nature of evangelicalism. Given Pentecostal and charismatic rhetoric of engagement with the Powers, it would be unwise to remain at the level of individual intercession, and not advance to the genuine work of prophetic intercession, being the intercessor in the breach, standing for righteousness in the public square, engaging in the public conversation.

Expand the Role of the Diaconate

If there is a commitment to be salt and light in society, who within your church has the mandate to work on such engagement? And as small local churches do not have sufficient members that are literate in these issues, who are others in the city seeking to do the same? What forums are needed for discussion of these issues by members of your congregation and city?

Deacons are to handle the economics of church life. In the 21st Century, these need to become highly skilled. Have somebody read up on New Zealand and globalisation issues and present their findings to an economic diaconate in your church. Prepare discussions on how these relate to Biblical principles.

Discern where your deacons can be trained in cooperatives, economic redistribution, social work, economic theology and advocacy. A local church is unlikely to discern well on many public issues so needs to link with others be they denominational or across networks.

Political Process Engagement

At a wider level, in what political contexts can these issues be influenced? We have to understand the New Zealand political process is not ideal, but is based on party politics. How are these kinds of issues defined in New Zealand political party manifestos? What is the process of getting these party manifestos changed towards Kingdom values of community and nationally controlled and owned economics? What would be the process of forming a pressure group to work with your local politician or lobby government ministers or work with industry leaders?

Think Tanks

On the other hand, politicians are voices. Often they have little time for reflection on issues. To be effective they need support. The creation of national think-tanks that feed policy ideas to these politicians is needed. Such mini-institutions that engage scriptures with economics at a far more professional level than this simple booklet are critical. For example, Andrew Bradstock at *Otago University Theology Department* developed a Public Policy unit, now led by Professor David Tombs. In Auckland, *Maxim Institute* seeks to grapple with socio-political issues from a Christian perspective.

Social Movements

Yet even think-tanks will not capture the heart and mind of Kiwis. In the analysis of New Zealand Christian social engagement in *Spirit of Christ and the Postmodern City*,[2] and in the writings of sociologist, James Hunter, we indicate the critical nature of Christian-spawned social movements in bringing about political change. What are the current issues around which to crystallise social movements? What social movements are currently operating and how can these be informed by Christian values?

175

Create Church, Local and National Debate

Moving from a very individualised gospel to a gospel of the Kingdom of God, a gospel of Jubilee, the issues of cultural engagement multiply. The following are some issues that are worthy of discussion. Each church cannot do all things, so needs to identify two or three issues it can be passionate about. For mainstream denominations there are denominational structures through which many of these issues can be engaged.

For evangelicals, *ad hoc* structures have to be created. *VisionNetwork* has provided a vehicle for combined action through various task forces nationally. And there is always a question underlying such engagement as to how such issues enable communication of the gospel and conversion of people and the nation from sin.

For Pentecostals, there is, with each of the following, the question of how such issues relate to the presence of the Holy Spirit in his engagement as the one who hovers over creation. How do the out-workings of revival affect the transformation of the nation? How we work with him in such a process? I have developed a theology and strategic processes for this in *The Spirit of Christ and the Postmodern City*.

Poverty Issues

- **Family Breakdown**: Recent research by economists at WINZ have indicated that New Zealand would save millions, if families were strengthened. What are primary factors in the urbanisation process causing family breakdown? Identify the Biblical responses. What church actions can be taken? Who are the national Christian advocates for family and how can they assist your church in its local responses? You assist them in national responses? What governmental policy issues can be strengthened?
- **Elderly Care**: The best way to initiate discussion on this issue might be to review articles in the attached booklist by Waldegrave et. al.
- **Ameliorating Poverty Factors Among Ethnic Minorities**: Most churches are multi-ethnic, so ethnic leaders in the congregational structure need to bring research on the gaps, and barriers to closing these gaps. What Biblical principles affect responses and how do these critique government policies?
- **The New Poverty: Student Indebtedness**: Examine the implications of conversion of the right to education into a capitalist commodity over the last decades; the various political responses; and reflect on the Biblical principles that impact on those responses.

National control on assets, and the means and profits of production

- **Globalisation:** How does New Zealand reject US, IMF, TPPA and World Bank pressures to sell state assets, particularly national assets, land and means of production to foreign ownership.

- **Banking:** Should we require banks in New Zealand step by step to come under New Zealand ownership again? The excessive printing of money by banks as loans are created is escalating housing and land prices. You likely will need a banker or economist to try to understand these issues. How then should we be responding to the issues based on Biblical principle? Should we build off the social movement, *Positive Money* in the UK, to create a pressure group on parliamentarians to change this process?

- **Cooperative Ownership**: How do we encourage the formation of cooperatives and poor people banks in New Zealand that are not beholden to the global banking interests?

- **Foreign Ownership:** Review the scriptures that lead to the Biblical principle of not being subject to foreign nations. Can we reduce the percentage of foreign ownership of New Zealand companies, so that decisions are made in the national interest? New Zealand already has mechanisms to limit this when it is not in the national interest, but these are often circumvented. Review such processes by reviewing documentation by Statistics New Zealand on asset sales. You might begin by contrasting works by opposing camps – the businessmen who make money by bringing in foreign investment[3] and those who oppose globalisation.[4]

- **Land:** The soul needs to be connected to the land. To increase protections on New Zealand land from foreign ownership, how do we strengthen the laws and implementation of existing structures that limit ownership of productive land by foreign companies?

- **Forests:** Read some of Brueggemann's, *The Land*, and discuss the nature of home and land. The forests of New Zealand have always belonged to its people we have fought as to which of our people, but is there a rationale for them being owned by strangers? They are part of our *turangaewawae*. Should we re-establish ownership of New Zealand's forests? How do we revise protections of native forests to prevent them from being overplanted by income generating but vegetation-destroying and land-destroying pine forests? How do we work towards more efficient processes of protecting and harvesting native forests? What is the Christian input to current discussions about forming forest cooperatives? How should we require yearly increasing percentages of export logging to be turned into value added products prior to export? How rapidly can forestry cooperatives develop and buy back foreign-owned forest land?

Fair Trade vs Free Trade

- **Jobs:** Discuss how creating a context for all to have productive jobs is in line with the Biblical mandates. How can we replace protections of some industries that have struggled to survive against the overwhelming imports from China due to free trade agreements based on China's maintaining low wages and fixing its exchange rates? New Zealand has been proactive in training people for the creative industries. But job retraining has been a failure in most countries to replace a significant number of jobs lost to free trade agreements. Which kind of work in NZ has intrinsic value? One way to evaluate that is to analyse if the type of work is a zero sum game or a productive one. Multiplication of casinos ostensibly to create jobs is not in line with productive work as it is a zero sum game, and they are socially destructive. How can these be closed down? Discuss the local context and what can be done to encourage job creation.

- **Fair Trade:** Have someone read up on "Fair vs Free trade" and present their findings to the group or bring in someone from Trade Aid[5] to do this. Discuss how these relate to Biblical principles. Jane Kelsey's works have laid a foundation for national opposition to the latest trade agreements. Should you be involved in the activist movement to stop TPPA? Measure her expertise against the Biblical norms. An alternative positive analysis at ValueWalkStaff indicates the proposed positives of such an accord, so provides a balancing set of perspectives.

- **Migration:** Part of globalisation is increased migration. The scriptures have much to teach on welcoming migrants. Evaluate these against migration policies and actual migration realities.

Reflections on Hermeneutics

In this study we have taken ten simple Biblical principles of economics, and applied them at five levels of society. Has that proven a viable approach?

The first question is whether we have exegeted the scriptures validly. Do the principles capture the breadth of the maybe fifty Biblical principles we could have chosen? Have we interpreted their context accurately as they were used in their specific cultures? Have we integrated the themes adequately across the breadth of redemption history as seen in the Bible?

The second is one of interpretation into themes. Are these ten principles representative? Do these reflect the tenor of the whole of the scriptures. Is there a balance to the way they are developed. Are they confirmed as significant by other theologians throughout history.

Have we then engaged with some Kiwi economic issues in a valid manner? Since the issues are complex and the themes are simple is this even a reasonable approach to developing ethics? It will have become apparent throughout this study that we tend to move form a Biblical cluster of principles to an economic theme or theory and back. In doing so we have in essence created intermediate levels of theology related to land rights, cooperative economics and trade.

As stated at the outset, this study is theological but the technical elements of political economic decision-making in New Zealand are very complex. Thus many conclusions are open ended, and inadequate. The study is best perceived as an openings of conversation spaces, where Christian economists can perhaps far better refine the themes espoused in these discussions

Conclusion

Socialised Capitalism supported by a free society has roots in Christian values and is somewhat compatible with Christianity. We live within it and hence can affirm some of its blessings. But we are also called to critique it and constantly seek to regulate or modify its inherent greed and collective sinfulness. In this study we have attempted to apply ten Biblical principles to this environment as a way of opening up Christian engagement in creating *conversational spaces* in New Zealand with the rapidly changing technological economic domain.

This engagement becomes crucial as we gyrate from one economic crisis to another. Capitalism oscillates from boom to bust (Marx saw in this its eventual demise). We expect the next global bust to be more catastrophic than 2008, despite some tinkering subsequently by central banks and the *Bank for International Settlements in Switzerland* to decrease the levels of money expansion by banks, but it is unclear how catastrophic. It is clear though, that New Zealand is far from ready for this next season. It no longer has ownership of its banking sector and less and less of other sectors. It is following a classic pathway that I observed in the third world in the 1980's of selling assets to foreigners until the outflow of profits increasingly cripples capacity to expand internally.

Thus some results of the study include a call to local ownership of resources; for the church to create alternative cooperative banking systems; work to enable its people to access capital through cooperative processes; train in entrepreneurial fields of production, and regain ownership of their own means of production.

It is abundantly clear that the failure (though not lack of engagement) by the church in preventing the loss of sale of our critical national banking, forestry and housing assets in the 1990's,[6] in not succeeding at the forefront of defending our freedoms in various trade negotiations – this moral failure of the church is a great national tragedy that by default has allowed our nation to become vulnerable to the next season of global crisis and ongoing exploitation.

This work has not necessarily provided technical answers but sought to open up the moral implications in the questions: How do we move forward into bringing the principles of the Kingdom into the public economic square? How will grassroots movements back moral leaders into effective national dialogue on economic issues? How do we enable our Kiwi people and our church people to regain ownership of our production, housing, land and banking systems? How do we work with God to economically defend New Zealand in the midst of global economic warfare? How do we interpret to our people the role of God in the existing structures and when he judges their evil?

This book is a miniscule contribution to catalyse your action. Some are called to live quietly, working with their hands. Some need to build national movements of economic discipleship. And yet others need to engage in the governance issues of the nation.. The future of our nation is yours!

Of the making of books [on economics and theology] there is no end! –Solomon.

Appendices

This book is in continuous upgrading over the years. More extensive resources are available on www.urbanleaders.org/560CommEcon or www.economicdiscipleship.online. Join the *Kiwinomics* Facebook or *Economic Discipleship* Facebook pages for discussion and reactions, corrections, new directions, implications, discussion points, extensions, clarifications, innovations, artistic contributions, or patterns of multiplication.

Appendix 1: Economic Discipleship in your Church

The material in chapter 2-3 can be utilised to *preach a Biblical foundation* from the pulpit. As a quarter of Jesus teaching was about economic issues, this is a godly activity. When pastors have only one economic message – "give your tithe to the church", it is selfish, short-sighted and violates the mandate to train our flocks. *The Ten Principles of Economic Discipleship* are a useful resource for messages on a liberating pattern of teaching, week by week.

Deacons are meant to help with church economic issues and the poor. One or more need to be *assigned as deacons* in the church to help individuals and couples to put these principles in practice.

The materials in chapter 3 & 4 will be set out as a *Level 1 Economic Discipleship series of small group studies* for six weeks that can be used by everyone in the congregation. Some of them need to be supplemented by a *Seminar on Budgeting*. *Liberty Trust, CAP* and other organisations funded by the government have excellent materials for this.

A second set of materials grapple with economic systems and are intended for church leaders and believers who are leaders of society to engage in *structural change processes*. These *leadership level economic discipleship studie*s could be used to form the basis of discussion with leaders and thinkers in the church, leaders in business and non-Christian leaders in your community.

Creative Bible Studies for children in Bangkok, students in Nairobi, poor in Delhi or Manila, at the companion site to this book:
www.urbanleaders.org/560CommEcon/1BiblicalEconomics/Biblical Economics.html

http://www.urbanleaders.org/560CommEcon/ expands on the materials in this booklet and relates them to the global urban poor.

Appendix 2: Deacons: Economic Leadership

Most people think of a *deacon* as a servant, someone who gives out books at the door, tidies the chairs. Indeed in Cambodia, the translation of the word is of the lowliest *peon* (while the word *pastor* is a word translated as a leader of great authority). A brief reading of the calling, anointing, giftedness and lives of the first deacons, paints a very different story.

Deacons are skilled in redistribution of money from the rich to the poor. They are spiritual men and women (deaconesses), called to exercise those gifts in the management of the churches' funds for the poor. In 21st century jargon, they are economic experts, social workers, community development workers, budgeting advisors, with strong pastoral care for the needy. They must have good business heads and gifts of mercy.

The roles and qualities of deacons (Acts 6: 1-4 (follow the story of Stephen and Phillip); I Tim 3: 8-13) are well worth reflection. But these cannot simply be transported into the 21st century context. Theology first gets to grips with what the scriptures meant in their context. Then it asks how that can be translated into a dynamic equivalence in our culture and time. The following are some important questions for a congregation to grapple with:

- What would be the equivalent job description for deacons be in a 21st century city church? What giftedness and training would be needed?
- What kind of people have these character qualities in your church? What are they currently doing in ministry?
- How is your church currently engaged with the poor, the needy, the oppressed? How could your church open new dimensions of ministry that serve the needy in your community?
- What changes to the constitution, leadership definitions, and roles are needed to move the church into effective diaconal engagement?

Appendix 3: New Zealand Resources for Churches

Crown Financial Resources

Crown Financial Ministries, founded in 1976, is a US-based interdenominational ministry dedicated to equipping people to learn, apply, and teach biblical financial principles.   http://www.crown.org.nz/.

Liberty Trust

Liberty Trust is a Bible-based storehouse releasing God's community into greater financial liberty. More than 235 households and churches have received interest free mortgages and most are already debt free and able to give more freely of themselves and their finances to God's Kingdom. Think of the extra time and money you would have to fulfil the Great Commission with a debt free home or church!

God's people donate funds to Liberty Trust and are offered an interest-free mortgage, five times the total they have contributed after approximately 7-10 years. There are also options to contribute more and receive a loan offer sooner.

The standard seven-year loan term can either be increased by one year for every extra year you choose to wait to receive your loan, up to a maximum loan term of 15 years, or by higher contributions.

http://www.libertytrust.org.nz/

Christians Against Poverty

CAP is passionate about working with local churches across the nation to lift Kiwis out of debt, poverty and its causes -- into a life filled with hope and freedom. So have a look around, capture the vision, and find out how you can change lives!

http://www.capnz.org/

Appendix 4: Urban Leadership Foundation

Urban Leadership Foundation is **a virtual learning hub**:
- for networks of workers among the urban poor
- for city leadership teams that bring revitalisation to cities

Grassroots - facilitating development of leaders of urban poor movements

- **Story-telling gatherings** of leaders among the urban poor locally, regionally and globally.
- Developing a global network of **Urban Poor Trainers** to teach modules through **learning networks**, the web and cell phones.
- Establishing the **MA in Transformational Urban Leadership** for urban poor leaders with partnering tertiary institutions in five continents resulting in resourcing of faith communities and civil society organisations in cooperative economics, working with the marginalised, advocacy, engagement in land tenure struggles, community health, establishing slum educational processes, social entrepreneurship, church-planting

- **Publishing** best case practices of movement leadership, and theological reflection on these.

Fostering leadership teams to envision purposes for cities and nations

- Developing, delivering and reproducing training for city leaders and teams
- **Publishing** prophetic and strategic envisioning for cities as outcomes from these processes.

Catalysing cultural revitalisation for citywide transformation

- Spearheading deep thinking in the theory, theology and practice of citywide transformation within revitalisation movements.

Support leadership among the urban poor globally

- **Donations** for training, publishing, needs of urban poor workers may be sent through PayPal at http://www.urbanleaders.org/

- **Prayer:** Sign up for **newsletters at** http://www.urbanleaders.org/.

- **Train:** Browse the training options for urban poor leaders on http://www.urbanleaders.org/home/training and join a course.

- **Study:** Do your Master's degree in the slums. Visit http://www.matul.org/ to explore the MA in Transformational Urban Leadership.

Some Other Books by Viv Grigg

"How does the Spirit of Christ transform a postmodern city?"

The Spirit of Christ and the Postmodern City
develops a theology of revival that brings about
national transformation. It is a story-filled study of
the New Zealand revival from 1970-1996 and its
progressions towards transformation of New
Zealand culture and society. It is grounded in local
realities of Auckland as a postmodern city.

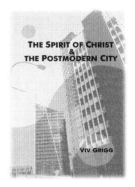

A must read for anyone in Christian leadership in
New Zealand, or seeking to expand the work of the
Holy Spirit into transformation, or eager to engage
the global megalopolises.
Available from Amazon, or Emeth Press.

Companion to the Poor

When he entered the Manila squatter settlement of Tatalon in 1979, Viv
Grigg and his team began to establish a Christian church among the slum
dwellers of its vast megalopolises. The challenge was to find a way that did
not treat people's spiritual needs in isolation from
their poverty.

This book is the enthralling story of how they met and
solved this problem, creating both a community of
faith and *new patterns of evangelical theology*. What has
begun is but the beginning of the founding of a
Christian community in a dark place.

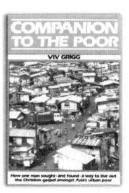

With over 15 printings, and translated into six
languages, its stories have been instrumental in the
mobilization of hundreds to work among the poor in
the urban slums globally.

Available from Amazon

Poor Wise Man Documentary

View the movie, *Poor Wise Man*, which documents some of Viv Grigg's
story and urban poor training. Available from: https://poorwiseman.vhx.tv/

Bibliography

Atherton, J. (1992). *Christianity and the Market: Social Christian Thought for Our Times.* London, SPCK.

Basel Committee on Banking Supervision. (2011). *Basel III: A global regulatory framework for more resilient banks and banking systems.* Switzerland: Bank for International Settlements.

Berger, Peter. (1987). *The Capitalist Revolution: Fifty Propositions About Prosperity, Equality and Liberty.* New York: Basic Books.

Berry, Wendell. (1981). *The Gift of Good Land: Further Essays Cultural and Agricultural.* North Point Press, San Francisco.

Boeke, J.H. (1953). *Economics and Economic Policy of Dual Societies.* Institute of Pacific Relations.

Brueggemann, Walter. (1977). *The Land.* Philadelphia: Fortress Press.

Brookes, W. (1986). Goodness and the GNP *Is Capitalism Christian?* Westchester, IL: Crossway Books.

Buchanan, C. and P. Hartley (2000). *Equity as a Social Goal.* Auckland, NZ Business Round Table.

Carroll, P., Casswell, S., Huakau, J., Howden-Chapman, P., & Perry, P. (2011). The widening gap: perceptions of poverty and income inequalities and implications for health and social outcomes. *Social Policy Journal Of New Zealand Te Puna Whakaaro*(37).

Castro, G. T. (1979). *Beyond Manila: Philippine Rural Problems in Perspective.* Ottawa: International Development Research Centre.

Catherwood, S. F. (1967). *The Christian in Industrial Society.* London, IVP.

Chafkin, M., & King, I. (2016, June 13). How Intel Makes a Chip. *Bloomberg Business Week.*

Chatterjee, S. and S. Birks, Eds. (2001). *The New Zealand Economy: Issues and Policies.* Palmerston North, Dunmore Press.

Clarke, M. (c1999). *Devolving forest ownership through privatisation in New Zealand.* New Zealand Forest Department. Retrieved from http://www.fao.org/docrep/X3030E/x3030e0a.htm

Clough, David, Richard Higginson and Michael Parsons. (2006). *Usury, Investment and the Sub-Prime Sector* http://www.christian-economists.org.uk/journal.htm

Clouse, R. G., Ed. (1984). *Wealth and Poverty: Four Opposing Evangelical American Perspectives.* Downers Grove, IL, IVP.

Coy, P. (2016, April 4). An Inconvenient Truth About... *Bloomberg Businessweek*, pp. 6-8.

Danaher, J., & William J. (1992). Healing Broken Bodies: The Missional Ecclesiology Behind J. H. Oldham's Middle Axioms. *Anglican Theological Review, 92*(2), 297-320.

Davies, William. (1974). *The Gospel and the Land.* Berkeley: University of California Press.

de Soto, Hernando. (2002). *The Other Path: The Economic Answer to Terrorism.* Translated by June Abbott. New York: Basic Books.

---. (2003). *The Mystery of Capital: Why Capitalism Triumphs in the West and Fails Everywhere Else.* Basic Books.

DK Publishing. (2012). *The Economics Book: Big Ideas Simply Explained* (Kindle ed.). New York: DK Publishing.

Dyrness, William. (1982). *Let the Earth Rejoice.* Manila, Philippines: Institute for Studies in Asian Church and Culture.

Eckert, Ross D. (1979). *The Enclosure of Ocean Resources: Economics and the Law of the Sea.* Stanford, CA: Hoover Institution Press, Stanford University.

Egbert, D. D., & Persons, S. (Eds.). (1952). *Socialism and the American Life* (Vol. 1). Princeton, New Jersey: Princeton University Press and London: Oxford University Press.

Eichbaum, C. (2001). Employment and Unemployment Policy Options in a Market Economy. *The New Zealand Economy: Issues and Policies*. S. Chatterjee and S. Birks. Palmerston North, Dunmore Press.

Ellul, Jacques. (1964). *The Technological Society*. NY, Random House, Vintage Books.

---. (1997). *The Meaning of the City*. Greenwood, SC: Attic Press.

Foster, Richard. (1997). *Freedom of Simplicity*. New York: HarperCollins.

Fowler, J. W. (1981). *Stages of Faith*. San Francisco: Harper and Row.

Frank, Andre Gunner. (1966). The Underdevelopment of Development. *Monthly Review Press*.

Galbraith, John Kenneth. (1981). *The Nature of Mass Poverty.*: Penguin.

Gheddo, P. (1989). *Why Is the Third World Poor?* : Greenhaven Press.

Glasser, Arthur. (1986). *The Kingdom and Mission*. Fuller Theological Seminary course syllabus.

Goodwin, M., & Burr, D. E. (2012). *Economix: How our Economy Works (and doesn't Work)*. New York: Abrams Comic Arts.

Goudzwaard, Bob, and Harry de Lange. (1994). *Beyond Poverty and Affluence: Towards an Economy of Care*. Grand Rapids: Eerdmans.

Grant, G. (1987). *Bringing in the Sheaves: Transforming Poverty into Productivity*. Fort Worth, TX, Dominion Press.

---. (1986). *In the Shadow of Plenty*. Fort Worth, TX, Dominion Press.

Green, D. P. (1996). *From Welfare State to Civil Society*, N.Z. Business Round Table.

Greer, Peter and Phil Smith. (2009). *The Poor Will Be Glad*. Grand Rapids: Zondervan.

Griffith, Brian. (1984). *The Creation of Wealth: A Christian's Case for Capitalism*. London: Hodder & Stoughton.

---. (1985). *Monetarism and Morality: A Response to the Bishops*. London, Centre for Policy Studies.

---. (1989). *Morality and the Market Place: Christian Alternatives to Capitalism and Socialism*. London: Hodder & Stoughton.

Grigg, Viv. (1983). *The Lifestyle and Values of Servants*. Auckland: Urban Leadership Foundation.

---. (1985/2004). Biblical Reflections on the Kingdom of God, Land and Land Rights. Auckland: Urban Leadership Foundation.

---. (2000). *Creating an Auckland Business Theology*. P.O. Box 20-524, Auckland, Urban Leadership Foundation.

---. (2010). *Companion to the Poor*. Auckland: Urban Leadership Foundation originally Abatross: Sydney (1984).

---. (2009a). *The Spirit of Christ and the Postmodern City: Transformative Revival Among Auckland's Evangelicals and Pentecostals*. Lexington, KY: Emeth Press and Auckland: Urban Leadership Foundation.

---. (2009b). Transformational Conversations: Hermeneutic for a Postmodern City *The Spirit of Christ and the Postmodern City: Transformative Revival Among Auckland's Evangelicals and Pentecostals*. Lexington, KY: Asbury: Emeth Press and Auckland: Urban Leadership Foundation.

Hagen, E. E. (1971). How Economic Growth Begins: A Theory of Social Change. In F. J. & R. Gable (Eds.), *Political Development and Social Change* (2nd ed.). New York: Wiley.

---. (1971). Personality and Entrepreneurship: How Economic Growth Begins: A Theory of Social Change. In J. L. Finkle & R. W. Gable (Eds.), *Political Development and Social Change*. New York: Wiley & Sons.

Hanks, T. (1983). God So Loved the Third World: The Biblical Vocabulary of Oppression. Maryknoll: Orbis.

Harris, Maria. (1996). *Proclaim Jubilee*. Louisville, Kentucky: Westminster.

Henderson, P. and J. Fox (2008). Proletarians of the World Unite. *Silent Legacy*. Auckland, Maxim Institute: pp. 151-164.

Hengel, Martin. (1998). *Property and Riches in the Early Church*. Philadelphia: Fortress Press.

Hobson, John. (1894/1928). *The Evolution of Modern Capitalism.*

Hodge, I. (1986). *Baptized Inflation: A Critique of "Christian" Keynesianism.* Tyler, TX, Institute for Christian Economics.

Hunter, J. D. (2010). *To Change the World: The Irony, Tragedy, and Possibility of Christianity in the Late Modern World:* Oxford University Press.

International Budget Partnership. (2016). *2015 Open Budget Survey.* Retrieved from http://www.internationalbudget.org/opening-budgets/open-budget-initiative/open-budget-survey/

International Labour Organization. (2006). *Guidelines on the formation of self help groups for families of working children.* Cambodia: International Labour Organization Retrieved from http://www.ilo.org/asia/whatwedo/publications/WCMS_108268/lang--en/index.htm

International Trade Forum Magazine. (2016). Fair Trade. *International Trade Forum Magazine.* Retrieved from http://www.tradeforum.org/fair-trade/

Jacobs, Jane. (1984). Cities and the Wealth of Nations. *The Atlantic Monthly* (Mar/Apr 1984).

Kagawa, Toyohiko. (1936). *Brotherhood Economics.* New York and London, Harper and Brothers.

Keeley, Brian. (2016). Income Inequality: The Gap between Rich and Poor. *OECD INSIGHTS.* Paris: OECD. Retrieved from http://dx.doi.org/10.1787/9789264246010-en

Kelsey, Jane. (1999). *Reclaiming the Future: New Zealand and the Global Economy.* Wellington, Bridget Williams Books.

---. (2013). *Hidden Agendas: What We Need to Know about the TPPA* Bridget Williams Books.

---. (2015). *The Fire Economy.* Wellington: Bridget Williams Books.

Kiare, Michael T. (2001). *Resource Wars.* New York: Henry Holt and Co.

Kohlberg, L. (1981). *The Philosophy of Moral Development:* Harper and Row.

Kuyper, A. (1991). *The Problem of Poverty.*

Latourette, Kenneth. (1953/1975). *History of Christianity, 2 vols.* New York: Harper and Row.

Lausanne Occasional Papers. (1980). *Christian Witness to the Urban Poor #22,* Lausanne Committee for World Evangelization, PO Box 1100, Wheaton, Illinois 60187, USA.

Laussane Committee on World Evangelization. (2004). Business As Mission. *Occasional Paper*(59).

Ledgerwood, J. (1999). *Microfinance Handbook: An Institutional and Financial Perspective.* Washington: The International Bank for Reconstruction and development/World Bank.

Levine, M. (2015). Kiwis view economic issues (44%) as biggest problem for NZ. . *Roy Morgan Research.*

Locke, J. (2009). Works of John Locke: Including Two Treatises of Government, An Essay Concerning Human Understanding and more, Amazon Kindle Edition.

Mackenzie, Alistair, Wayne Kirkland, and Annette Dunham. (2002). *Soulpurpose.* Christchurch: NavPressNZ.

Mackenzie, Alistair. (1997). *Faith at Work.* Master's Thesis. Dunedin, University of Otago.

Margolis, R. (2008). New Zealand Cooperatives as Religion. Retrieved from http://www.nz.coop/cooperatives-as-religion

Marx, Karl. (1974). Historical Materialism Summarized. In Etzioni & Etzioni (Eds.), *Social Change.*

Marx, Karl and Fredrich Engels. (1848). *The Communist Manifesto.* http://www.anu.edu.au/polsci/marx/classics/manifesto.html#c1r2

Maslow, A. H. (1954). *Motivation and Personality.* New York, Harper and Row.

May, R. H. (1991). The Poor of the Land: A Christian Case for Land Reform. Maryknoll, Orbis Books.

Mayhew, Ray. (2016). *Embezzlement: The Corporate Sin of Contemporary Christianity.* Retrieved from http://relationaltithe.com/featured-resources /embezzlement-the-corporate-sin-of-contemporary-christianity/

McAlpine, T. H. (2003). *Facing the Powers: What Are the Options?* : Wipf & Stock Publishers.

McClelland, David C. (1964). Business Drive and National Achievement. *Harvard Business Review* XL, no. 4 (1964): 165-78.

McDowell, Derek et. al. (2014). *Israel: Five Views on People, Land and State.* Auckland: Castle Publishing.

McGavran, Donald A. (1970). *Understanding Church Growth.* Eerdmans.

McGibben, Bill. (2008). *Deep Economy.* St Martins Griffen.

McKinnon, M. (1998). Rural Restructuring: Environment and Development, 1961-1991. In Malcolm McKinnon, B. Bradley, & R. Kirkpatrick (Eds.), *New Zealand Historical Atlas* (pp. 97-98). Auckland: Bateman.

Milson, E. (2016). Banks Impose New Restrictions on Overseas Property Buyers(9 June). Retrieved from http://www.scoop.co.nz/stories/BU1606/S00263/banks-impose-new-restrictions-on-overseas-property-buyers.htm

Ministry of Foreign Affairs and Trade. (2015). Trans-Pacific Partnership (TPP). New Zealand Government. Retrieved from https://www.mfat.govt.nz/en/trade/free-trade-agreements/free-trade-agreements-concluded-but-not-in-force/tpp/

Moore, Mike. (2003). *A World Without Walls.* Cambridge: University Press.

Myrdal, G. (1972). *Asian Drama: An Inquiry into the Poverty of the Nations* (abridged edn.). UK: Allen Lane.

National Conference of Catholic Bishops. (1986). *Economic Justice for All.* Washington: United States Catholic Conference.

Nelson, B. (1969). *The Idea of Usury: From Tribal Brotherhood to Universal Brotherhood:* University of Chicago Press.

North, D. C. (2005). *Understanding the Process of Economic Change.* New Jersey, Princeton University Press.

North, G. (1986). *Honest Money: Biblical Principles of Money and Banking.* Fort Worth, Texas, Dominion Press.

Novak, Michael. (2000). *The Spirit of Democratic Capitalism.* New York: Madison Books.

O'Callaghan, J. (1834). *Usury, Funds, and Banks: Or Lending at Interest.* Burlington.

Ohmae, Kenichi. (1991). *The Borderless World: Power and Strategy in the Interlinked Economy.* NY: Harper Collins.

Orange, Claudia. (1987). *The Treaty of Waitangi.* Allen and Unwin, Port Nicholson Press.

Payne, G. (2016). *Trade and Keep it in the Ground Letter* (July 9). Retrieved from https://ahimsa2015.wordpress.com/2016/05/19/trade-and-keep-it-in-the-ground-letter/

Pearce, Fred. (2012). *The Land Grabbers.* Boston: Beacon Press.

Penk, Alex (2008). *Is it Just Tax? The shaping of our society.* Auckland, Maxim Institute.

Perkins, H. (1979). *Shalom.* Paper presented at the Christian Conference of Asia, Singapore.

Pieper, Josef. (1999). *Leisure, the Basis of Culture.* Translated by Gerald Malsbary. 50 ed. P.O. Box 2285, South Bend, Indiana 46680 - 2285: St Augustine Press.

Porter, Michael. (1990). *The Competitive Advantage of Nations.* New York: The Free Press.

Randerson, R. (1992). *Hearts and Minds: A Place for People in a Market Economy.* Wellington, Social Responsibility Commission of the Anglican Church.

---. (1987). *Christian Ethics and the New Zealand Economy.* Wellington, Department of Christian Education, Diocese of Wellington. New Zealand.

Richter, W. (2016). *Desperate Chinese Investors Flood US, Canadian Housing Markets, But Real Numbers Are Taboo* Vancouver: Wolf Street Retrieved from http://wolfstreet.com/2016/03/24/chinese-buyers-invade-vancouvers-housing-market-study/

Rosen, C., Case, J., & Staubus, M. (2005). *Equity: Why Employee Ownership is Good for Business.* Boston, MA: Harvard Business School Press.

Rostow, W. W. (1991). *The Stages of Economic Growth: A Non-Communist Manifesto* (3rd ed.). Cambridge: Cambridge University Press.

Ryken, L. (1987). *Work and Leisure in Christian Perspective.* Portland, OR: Multnomah Press.

Sachs, J. D. (2006). *The End of Poverty: Economic Possibilities for Our Time.* London: Penguin.

Santos, Milton. (1975) *The Shared Space: The Two Circuits of the Urban Economy in Underdeveloped Countries.* Translated from Portuguese edition by Chris Gerry. London and New York: Methuen.

Schor, J. B. (1992). *The Overworked American.* New York, Basic Books.

Schramm, Carl J. (2008). *Economic Fluidity: A Crucial Dimension of Economic Freedom.* The Heritage Foundation.

Schumacher, E.F. (1989). *Small Is Beautiful: Economics as If People Matter.* London: Abacus and NY: Harper Perennial.

Schweitzer, A. (1923/1961). *The Decay and the Restoration of Civilization.* London: Unwin Books.

Scrimgeour, F. (2008). *Economics, Faith and the 21ˢᵗ Century.* New Vision New Zealand, Vol III. B. Patrick. Auckland, Vision Network.

Sen, Armartya. (2000). *Development as Freedom.* Anchor Books.

Sheard, Murray. (1999). *Living Simply.* Auckland: Tear Fund and World Vision.

Sider, Ron, Ed. (1981). *Evangelicals and Development: Towards a Theology of Social Change.* Exeter, Paternoster.

---. (2005). *Rich Christians in an Age of Hunger.* London: Thomas Nelson.

Smith, A. (1776). *The Wealth of Nations.* Kindle Version.

Smithies, R., & Wilson, H. (Eds.). (1993). *Making Choices: Social Justice for Our Times.* Wellington: Dept. of Communications, Presbyterian Church of Aotearoa New Zealand.

Snyder, H. (1985). The Age of Jubilee. *A Kingdom Manifesto.* pg. 68-76.

Sombart, W. (1902). *Der moderne Capitalismus.* Germany: Dunker and Humblot.

Tawney, R.H. (2008). *Religion and the Rise of Capitalism.* Hesperides Press.

Thomas, S. (2008). Governing for the Good: What does it really mean? Auckland, Maxim Institute.

Thurow, L. (1996). *The Future of Capitalism: How Today's Forces will Shape Tomorrow's World.* 9 Atchison St., St Leonards, NSW 2065, Australia, Allen and Unwin.

Tippett, A. (1971). *People Movements in Southern Polynesia.* Chicago: Moody Bible Institute.

Torrey, A. I. (1979). *Biblical Economics.* Taebaek, Korea, Jesus Abbey.

Toynbee, A. (1972). *A Study of History* (First Abridged One volume Edition ed.). Oxford: Oxford University Press.

Treasury, N. Z. (2014). *Income from State Asset Sales as at May 2014.* Wellington: New Zealand Treasury Retrieved from http://www.treasury.govt.nz/government/assets/saleshistory

United Nations Development Program. (2016). *Human Development Report 2015: Work for Human Development.* Retrieved from http://report.hdr.undp.org/

UNHabitat. (2008-9). *State of the World's Cities: Harmonious Cities.* Nairobi: UNHabitat.

ValueWalk Staff. (2016). How These 12 TPP Nations Could Forever Change Global Growth. Retrieved from http://www.valuewalk.com/2015/10/tpp-draft/

van Lerven, Frank. (2016). *A Guide to Public Money Creation.* London: Positive Money.

Vermeersch, A. (1912). Usury. *The Catholic Encyclopedia from New Advent.* Retrieved from http://www.newadvent.org/cathen/15235c.htm

Waldegrave C. and P. King. (2003) "Social Capital, Social Networks, and Access to Employment." *New Zealand Population Review.* 29(1).

Waldegrave C and Pole N (2001) "Taking Our Opportunities: Social Cohesion and the Knowledge Divide in Aotearoa, New Zealand" in *The Proceedings of the Catching the Knowledge Wave Conference held in Auckland 1–3 August 2001, Theme Papers, Social Cohesion and the Knowledge Divide (Paper two)*.

Waldegrave C (1998) "Balancing the Three Es, Equality, Efficiency and Employment" *Social Policy Journal of New Zealand*, 10, June.

Waldegrave C (1997) "Superannuation: Income Adequacy, Affordability and Equity" in *The Proceedings of the New Zealand Retirement Savings Summit, May 29,30 1997*, Wellington, Inst. for International Research, Auckland

Waldegrave C.T. (1992) "The Family: Morality Versus Economic Reality" in Eds. Novitz D.& Willmott B. *New Zealand in Crisis*, Government Print.

Waldegrave C.T. (1991) "Full Employment, Equity, Participation and a Viable New Zealand Economy" in Ed. Pelly R. *Towards a Just Economy.* , The Combined Chaplains' Victoria University of Wellington.

Waldegrave C.T. & Frater P. (eds). (1991) *The National Government Budgets of the First Year of Office: A Social Assessment.* A report to Sunday Forum prepared by the Family Centre and Business & Economic Research Ltd (BERL).

Waldegrave C.T. (1991) "Budget '91: Monetarist Dream Citizen's Nightmare". *Social Work Review* 4,2 & 3 pp 33-34.

Waldegrave C. & Coventry R. (1987) *Poor New Zealand: An Open Letter on Poverty*. Platform Publishing.

Waldegrave C.T. (1984) "Who pays for the Economic Reconstruction?" in *Economic Summit Conference Proceedings and Conference Papers Vol.2*. Government Print.

Wallerstein, I. (2004). *World Systems Analysis: An Introduction.* Duke University Press.

Webb, S. H. (2007). New Theology, Old Economics. *First Things*. (212) 627-1985 • ft@firstthings.com • 35 East 21st Street, 6th floor, New York, NY 10010, The Institute on Religion and Public Life.

Weber, M. (2010). *The Protestant Work Ethic and the Spirit of Capitalism* (T. Parsons, Trans.). London: Oxford.

Wilkinson, Bryce. (2014). *New Zealand's Global Links: Foreign Ownership and the Status of New Zealand's Net International Investment.* Auckland: The New Zealand Initiative.

Wilkinson, Richard, and Kate Pickett. (2007). *The Spirit Level: Why More Equal Societies Almost Always Do Better.* London: Allen Lane.

Wilson, J. (2010). *Short History of Post-Privatisation in New Zealand.* Wellington: New Zealand Treasury.

Wogaman, J. P. (1986). *Economics and Ethics: A Christian Enquiry.* Philadelphia, Fortress Press & London: SCM Press.

Woodberry, Robert (2012). The Missionary Roots of Liberal Democracy. *American Political Science Review*, 106, pp 244-274. doi:10.1017/S0003055412000093.

World Economic Forum. (2015). *The Global Competitiveness Report 2014–2015.*

Wright, Chris J. H. (1990) *God's People in God's Land: Family, Land and Property in the Old Testament*, Exeter: Paternoster Press.

Yunus, M. (1999). *The Grameen Bank.* Scientific American (November 1999): 114-119.

Index

Endnotes

Introducing the Conversationalists

[1] Randerson (1987, 1992), Charles Waldegrave (1987,1989, 1991), Ruth Smithies & Helen Wilson (eds.) (1993).

[2] www.matul.org

[3] There are many Kiwi-related resources husbanded by Alistair McKenzie at: http://www.faithatwork.org.nz/index.htm.

[4] (Grigg, 2009b).

[5] The *Kingdom of God* is the same as the *Kingdom of Heaven* in Matthew. As he was writing to the Jews, he could not use the word YHWH for God, as it was too sacred.

[6] The name Kiwinomics has no links to previous uses of the term, but happened on a restaurant napkin. Alan Ferguson has a section of his blog with that name alansfridgedoor.com, and a couple of others have used it in nws articles or wordpress blogs..

[7] Danaher, W. J., 1992.

[8] The conversation of this book is expanded to the global urban poor at: www.urbanleaders.org/560CommEcon.

Chapter 1: Responding to the Issues of Our Time

[1] Psa 84:11.

[2] Gen 26:1,12.

[3] Levine, 2015.

[4] Knight & Laugeson, 2005.

[5] Penk, 2008.

[6] Mark 4:19.

[7] Temple, 1942: 29-34.

[8] Max Weber, 2010.

[9] Kuyper, 1991.

[10] Hengel, 1998.

[11] See for example, Hanks (1983) for an excellent Biblical exegesis on oppression, with a little Marxist twist at the end.

[12] Novak, 2000:18. He does the same as the liberationists by letting an overarching economic schema capture the Biblical exegesis – in his case Democratic Capitalism.

Chapter 2: The Genesis of Economics

[1] It is beyond the scope of these studies to discuss the source of the philosophy and theology of Genesis 1 nor the theories of P and Q and other theses that have been put forward over the last century as to the authorship and exilic or post-exilic integration of these.

[2] Whether of fundamentalist belief in the processes of creation in seven days being seven actual days or more modern perspectives on evolutionary creative forces across the aeons, nearly all Christians recognise these generic statements about the God of creation who continues to sustain creation, as foundational to Christian doctrine.

[3] Gen 3:16-19.

[4] Deut 8:17, Prov 30:9.

[5] Prov 23:5.

[6] Ecc 5:11.

[7] Prov 11:28.
[8] Lev 26.
[9] Lev 25:23.
[10] Lev 26.
[11] Deut 8:18-20, Micah 2:1-5.
[12] Gen 2:7.
[13] Gen 1:26-28.
[14] Gen 1:27.
[15] Sider, pg. 60.
[16] Psa 65:11-13.
[17] Grigg, 2004, ch. 3.
[18] Based on Greer (2009).
[19] Psa 15:5.
[20] Ezek 18:8, 13, 17.
[21] Neh. 5:1–12.
[22] Gen 31.
[23] Gen. 22:14.
[24] Exod 16.
[25] I Kings 17:1-6.
[26] Gen 14:20; Heb 7:6.
[27] 2 Chron 31:5.
[28] Amos 4:4; Mal 3:8-10.

Chapter 3: Jubilee Justice

[1] Luke 4:18.
[2] Howard Snyder, to whom many of us are indebted for his integration of church growth and Kingdom principles, in *Kingdom Manifesto* (1985), gives a serious theological derivation of this concept.
[3] http://www.faithatwork.org.nz/index.htm
[4] Ecc 10:18; 11:6.
[5] Lev 25:1-7.
[6] Lev 25:8-17.

Chapter 4: Economic Jesus

[1] Luke 19.8.
[2] Matt 10:24, 25.
[3] John 8:31.
[4] John 14:21.
[5] Luke 17:21.
[6] Phil 2:5-8.
[7] Mark 1:15.
[8] Acts 10:38.
[9] Matt 12:28.
[10] Luke 10:18.
[11] 1 Cor. 15:26; Heb 2:14.
[12] Matt 25:34.
[13] Isa 42:3.
[14] John 12:47.
[15] Dan 2:31-35.
[16] Heb 6:5.

[17] 2 Cor 1:22.

[18] 1 Cor. 15:50.

[19] 1 John 4:4.

[20] Matt 25:41.

[21] John 16:13

[22] 1 Cor 13:12.

[23] Rom 12:2.

[24] Rom 8:21.

[25] Mark 16:15.

[26] Rom 14:12.

[27] Luke 6:34.

[28] Rev 18.

[29] Rev 18:11-18.

[30] 2 Thes 2:2-11.

[31] Mark 16:15, Luke 10:9.

[32] Luke 4:18.

[33] Matt 28:19-20.

[34] This is not a crusade or Jihad but a battle for the soul, the Spirit (Matt 10:34-39). Similarly, Jihad can be interpreted as the inner battle for righteousness rather than violence.

[35] Johnson, Todd, (2012) *The Demographics of Christian Martyrdom.* www.gordonconwell.edu/.../TheDemographicsofChristianMartyrdom.pdf

[36] II Corinthians 5:19, 20.

[37] Luke 14:26; Mark 10:34.

[38] Luke 14:26; 9:23.

[39] Luke 12:33; 14:33.

[40] Luke 9:57,58.

[41] Mark 1:16ff; 10:17ff, 28ff.

[42] Mark 10: 28, 29.

[43] Matt 6:25-34.

[44] Acts 4:32-34.

[45] Luke 8:2; 10:38.

[46] Mark 7:9; Mark 12:41; Matt 6:2; 25:40.

[47] Acts 28:31.

[48] 1 Cor 9:22, 23.

[49] 2 Cor 6:10.

[50] Phil 4:12.

[51] 1 Corinthians 7:29, 30.

[52] Isa 42:1-4; 49:1-6; 50:4-9; 52:13-53:12.

[53] 2 Cor 6:2

[54] Snyder, 1985 pg. 70.

[55] Rom 8:21.

[56] Mark 16:15.

[57] Rom 8:19, 20.

[58] Luke 2:24.

[59] Rom 8:38-39.

[60] Jam 2:5.

[61] Mark 10:25.

[62] Matt 25:31-46.

[63] Matt 6:14.

[64] Luke 18:24.

[65] Luke 12:15; Eph 5:5; Ex 20:17.

66 Col 3:5.
67 1 Cor 5:11.
68 1 Tim 6:10.
69 Luke 16:33.
70 Prov 18:10.
71 Luke 16:19-31.
72 1 John 3:16.
73 Matt 6:24.
74 Matt 13:22.
75 Rom 14:17.
76 John 9:4; 4:34; 5:17.
77 Mark 3:14.
78 Matt 9:36-39.
79 Ryken, 1987, pg. 87.
80 Mark 2:27.

Chapter 5: Jubilee and Economics in the Early Church

1 Matt 26:9.
2 Acts 2:46.
3 1 John 3:17.
4 James 1:9.
5 1 Tim 6:6-8.
6 Matt 6:25-33.
7 Acts 28:23,31
8 1 Thes 4:11,12.
9 Acts 20:35.
10 Matt 9:37,38.
11 1 Tim 5:18.
12 Matt 6:25-33.
13 1 Tim 5:17.
14 Matt 6:11.
15 Rom 14:5-6.
16 1 Cor 9:13-14.
17 Phil 4:14,15.
18 Penk, 2008.
19 Thomas 2008.
20 I Timothy 6:6-8.
21 Grigg, 1983.
22 Sheard, 1999.

Ten Principles of Economic Discipleship

1 I Tim 5:8.
2 1 Tim 5:8.
3 Luke 4:18, Acts 2:42-44
4 1 Thes 4:11.
5 Matt 6:24-33.
6 Luke 12:33.
7 Luke 14:33.
8 1 Cor 9:22.
9 1 Tim 6:6-8.

[10] 2 Cor 8,9.
[11] John 8:32.
[12] Luke 12:33, 14:33
[13] 1 Tim 5:8.

Chapter 6: Biblical Financial Principles

[1] Gen 1:1, Jn 1:1-3.
[2] Gen 14:22, Psa 24:1-2.
[3] Rom 8:32, Phil 4:19
[4] Prov 3:5, 16:3, 19:21, 24:3.
[5] Prov 24:27.
[6] Luke 12:42, Luke 16:1-9, 1 Cor 4:1,2.
[7] I Pet 4:10.
[8] Ray Mayhew, 2016.
[9] I Tim 5:8; 2 Cor 12:14; Mark7:9-13.
[10] Matt 17:26; 22:21; Rom 13:6.
[11] Rom 13:8.
[12] Prov 22:7.
[13] Prov 3:27, 28.
[14] Lev 25:36.
[15] Prov 19:17.
[16] Luke 6:34,35.
[17] Psa 112:5.
[18] Lev 25:26; Deut 24:10-14.
[19] Lev 25:10.
[20] Prov 6:1-5; 11-15; 20:16; 27:13.
[21] Prov 22:26,27.
[22] Ex 22:25, Deut 23:19-20
[23] Nelson, 1969, pg. 3.
[24] O'Callaghan, 1834, loc. 1166.
[25] Sombart was of equal significance in the development of historical economic sociology as his peer, Max Weber. But his fascist and anti-Jewish perspectives have left him with little recognition (Grundmann, R., & Stehr, R., 2001). When it comes to his extensive analysis of the historic roots of Capitalism his work on Imperialism (1902) is the classic source.
[26] Sombart, 1902.
[27] Vermeersch, 1912.
[28] Resolution 213, Investment Ethics, GBPHB, 2006.
[29] II Cor 6:14.
[30] II Timothy 2:2-6.
[31] Ecc 3:1-9.
[32] Prov 6:8.
[33] Prov 21:20.
[34] Prov 27:23-27; 14:16.
[35] Prov 15:27; 28:25.
[36] Prov 13:22.

Chapter 7: The Cooperative Principle

[1] Keeley, 2016.

2 Latourette, 1953/1975.

3 The following paragraphs are based on the New Zealand Cooperatives Association website.

4 McGavran in early versions of *Understanding Church Growth* popularized extensive research by Bishop Pickett in India.

5 www.matul.org

6 International Labour Organization, 2006.

7 Galbraith, John Kenneth, c1980.

8 ILO, 2006

9 Ledgerwood, 1999.

Chapter 8: The Kingdom of God, Land and Land Ownership

1 The scriptures have little to say about corporate ownership or intellectual property rights per se. Which raises the hermeneutical question as to the potential to realistically extend the Biblical ownership principles into these domains. The derivative theologies of property rights have a long history through the British legal system, and on into international law. Those principles can be confirmed. Their application requires exploring specific business ethical practices in each of these areas of ownership.

2 This chapter is a reduced and updated version of a booklet published in 1985 by the same title. A power point presentation may be accessed at:

http://www.authorstream.com/Presentation/vivgrigg-2509956-theology-land-rights/

3 Tippett, A. (1971). *People Movements in Southern Polynesia*. Chicago: Moody Bible Institute.

4 Over thirty years of teaching on a theology of land rights, I have reworked Brueggemann's approach of three movements in his classic, *The Land* (1977).

5 Martens 1981, pg. 97.

6 Wright, C. 1990.

7 Gen 1:4,10,12,18,21,24,31.

8 Gen. 1:12,22,28.

9 Gen 3:17-19.

10 Dyrness 1982:24.

11 Deut 8:17,18.

12 Deut 8:7-10.

13 Dyrness 1982 pg. 30.

14 Brueggemann, 1977, pg. 79.

15 Gen 50:5-14.

16 Martens 1981, pg.102.

17 Josh 13-19.

18 Orange 1987:115.

19 Prov 23:11.

20 Brueggemann, 1977.

21 Lev 19:29; Num 35:29ff.

22 Deut 28.

23 Isa 6:8.

24 Mic 2:2.

25 Deut 24:6; Ex 22:25.

26 Neh 9:36-38.

27 The issue of the restoration of Israel and the land disputes in Palestine is outside the mandate of this study. Other New Zealanders have debated this well (McDowell et. al., 2014).

Part 3: Discipleship of Economic Systems

1 Goodwin and Burr, 2012.

2 *The Big Book of the Economy*, DK Publishing, 2012.
3 Frank Scrimgeour is a Professor of Economics at the University of Waikato Management School. A leading environmental economist, he has contributed to regional, Māori and national policymaking.
1 Graph from the 2015 Open Budget Survey.

Chapter 9: Biblical Principles and Political Economy

2 De Soto, 2003.
3 World Economic Forum, 2015.
4 International Budget Partnership, 2016.
5 Moore, 1993, pg. 8.
6 Carl J. Schramm, 2008.
7 United Nations Development Program, 2016.
8 Brookes, 1986.
9 Grigg, 1981.
10 Kelsey, 1999.

Chapter 10: Kingdom and Capitalism

1 This greater income inequality has seen New Zealand move into 18th place out of 25 in the OECD in terms of income inequality from 1982 to 2004 (Ministry of Social Development 2007). Over the preceding two decades New Zealand experienced the largest growth in inequalities in the OECD (2000 figures), moving from 2 Gini coefficient points below the OECD average to 3 Gini points above (Ministry of Social Development 2007:45-46). One indication of the impact of these inequalities has been that relative poverty rates, including child poverty rates, have increased (Carroll et. al., 2011).
2 Eph 6:11,12; II Cor 10:3-5.
3 There is a long historic debate as to the nature of the Powers, where recent notables include Wink, Yoder and are well summarised in Tom McAlpine (2003).
4 Isa 42:1-4.
5 Hobson, 1894.
6 These principles are fleshed out in our Masters level course on *Land Rights and Advocacy*, that grapples with an evangelical Christian engagement in working with slum-dwellers in obtaining land tenure for slum dwellers.(http://www.urbanleaders.org/655LandRights).
7 www.positivemoney.org
8 Frank van Lerven, 2016.
9 Berger, 1987; Novak, 1982.
10 J.H. Boeke, 1953.
11 Perkins, 1979.
12 Castro, 1979.
13 See, for example "Rural Restructuring" in the *New Zealand Historical Atlas* (McKinnon, 1998).
14 James 5:1-6.
15 UNHabitat, 2009.
16 Ex 22:25.
17 Lev 19:9,10.
18 Wilkinson, 2014 pg. 5.
19 Wilson, J., 2010.
20 Clarke, M. c1999, pg. 9.
21 Leahy, 2014.
22 Richter, 2016.
23 Milson, 2016.

[24] Figure 14: Source: Balance of Payments, Key Statistics 7.04 - Value of principal exports (excl. re-exports). Statistics NZ. Courtesy wakupkiwi.com.
[25] Matt 25:41.
[26] Gheddo, 1989.
[27] Matt 23:8-12.
[28] Ezek 16:49.
[29] 1 Tim 6:8.
[30] Col. 3:5.
[31] Matt 6:25-32.
[32] Psa 112:5.

Chapter 11: Creativity, Innovation and Entrepreneurship

[1] Chafkin, M., & King, I., 2016, June 13.
[2] The flip side of the argument is that if the gospel does not impact a growing percentage of New Zealanders, the innovative, and creative nature of God inherent in the birthing of our culture (by shiploads of Methodist and Baptist non-conformists in Auckland in 1862 and in other cities by Presbyterians and Anglicans) will decline.
[3] Chartered Accountants Australia and New Zealand, 2015, pg. 6.
[4] ibid.
[5] Watson, 2016 pg. 5.
[6] McLelland, 1964; Everett E. Hagen, 1971.
[7] Weber, 1947.
[8] Marx, 1974.
[9] Mark 7:20-22.
[10] Rom 16:17.
[11] Rom 12:2.
[12] McLelland, 1964, pg. 176.
[13] ibid., pg. 177.
[14] Isa 32:17.
[15] Woodberry, 2012.
[16] Toynbee, 1972.
[17] Hall, 1995, pg. 32.
[18] Kohlberg, 1981.
[19] Maslow, 1954.
[20] Fowler, 1981.
[21] Foucault, 1972.
[22] Test yourself with the analysis at:
www.empretec.unctad.org/wpcontent/uploads/2015/ 09/EG_eng.compressed.pdf
[23] Lausanne Committee on World Evangelization, 2004.
[24] e.g. Rosen, 2005.

Chapter 12: Kingdom, Socialism and Marxism

[1] Hanks, 1983.
[2] Randerson 1987, pg. 21.
[3] Hanks, 1983.
[4] Matt 5:1-12.
[5] James 1:9.
[6] Philemon 15, Matt 23:8-10.
[7] Acts 4:32)
[8] Luke 19:8.

9 I John 3:16.

10 Lev 25:23.

11 I Sam 24:6.

12 Psa 75:7.

13 Rom 12:19, 24.

14 This is the field of *Advocacy and Community Organization* that we teach as a course in our *MA in Transformational Urban Leadership* globally.

15 II Pet 3:9.

Chapter 13: Discipling the Global Economy

1 II Cor 10:3-5. I do not wish to denigrate the hidden prayers of the saints as they cry out to God, and the power of such prayer to change the course of history. Yet in *The Spirit of Christ and the Postmodern City* (Grigg, 2009a, ch. 13), I have sought to demonstrate how the Biblical model of the prophet and intercessor is one who stands in between God and the powers, stands in the public place of conflict. This is the activist intercessor. In modern society, such a person must be well educated, and develop credibility socially and organisationally.

2 Kelsey, 1999, pg. 189.

3 Michael T Kiare, 2001.

4 Fred Pearce, 2012.

5 Eckert, 1979.

6 Rev 17:1, 2.

7 17:3; 18:2.

8 Daniel 7:20.

9 18:3,4.

10 18:24.

11 Basel Committee on Banking Supervision III, 2011, pg. 58.

12 Moore, 2003, pg. 13.

13 Eph 1:21; 3:10; 6:11,12. See Tom McAlpine's *Facing the Powers* (2003) for a well-reasoned treatment of four historic Biblical theological approaches to "the Powers".

14 Porter, 1990.

15 Coy, 2016.

16 WikiLeaks, *The US strategy to create a new global legal and economic system TPP, TTIP, TISA.* https://www.youtube.com/watch?v=OwShmx7sXUU For an establishment statement of the same, *Obama races to cement trade pact*, Los Angeles Times, May 27, 2016, pg. 1. Where he speaks of the US important strategic benefits, indicating the exclusion of China.

17 Payne, 2016.

18 http://itsourfuture.org.nz/tppa-text/.

19 International Trade Forum Magazine, 2016.

20 Jacobs, Jane, 1984.

Chapter 14: Economic Discipleship in Action

1 Grigg, 1985.

2 Grigg, 2009a.

3 Wilkinson, 2014.

4 See graphs on wakeupkiwi.com for example.

5 http://www.tradeaid.org.nz

6 Though not a lack of voice from the mainstream church leadership - see for example Randerson (1987, 1992), or Charles Waldegrave (1987,1989, 1991), Ruth Smithies & Helen Wilson (eds.) (1993).

43874162R00123

Made in the USA
San Bernardino, CA
30 December 2016